Also edited by E. O. Parrott

The Penguin Book of Limericks
Limerick Delight
How to Become Ridiculously Well-Read in One Evening
Imitations of Immortality

Compiled and edited by E. O. Parrott

HOW TO BECOME ABSURDLY WELL-INFORMED ABOUT THE FAMOUS AND INFAMOUS

A Collection of Brief Biographies

VIKING

VIKING

Penguin Books Ltd, 27 Wrights Lane, London W8 5Tz (Publishing and Editorial)
and Harmondsworth, Middlesex, England (Distribution and Warehouse)
Viking Penguin Inc., 40 West 23rd Street, New York, New York 10010, U.S.A.
Penguin Books Australia Ltd, Ringwood, Victoria, Australia
Penguin Books Canada Ltd, 2801 John Street, Markham, Ontario, Canada L3R 1B4
Penguin Books (N.Z.) Ltd, 182–190 Wairau Road, Auckland 10, New Zealand

First published 1987

Typeset in Lasercomp Plantin
Printed in Great Britain by
Richard Clay Ltd, Bungay, Suffolk

British Library Cataloguing in Publication Data available

For my grandson, Ben,
in the hope that he may surpass
all these in fame and fortune

CONTENTS

PROLOGUE

The Diary of an Editorial Nobody

Tuesday

After working hard all day I went downstairs at teatime, and told Carrie that I had finished the book. She didn't even bother to ask: 'What book?' but merely said she supposed that I had had the usual trouble with the Introduction. I told her: 'No. Not at all.'

'I find that very hard to believe,' she said. 'We all know only too well that you find that the hardest part. Why, a good introduction seems to take you almost as long as the book itself. What sort of introduction is it this time? I hope it isn't one of those jokey ones like you do sometimes.'

It was at this point I had to confess that I had only just begun the thing.

'Then it's no wonder you've had no trouble with it,' sneered Carrie, 'though how you can say you've finished the book, I do not know; and now, if you'd care to get all those papers away, I'd like that table for tea.'

I said she could, and then added, rather wittily, that she might prefer a ham sandwich. The trouble with Carrie is that she has no sense of humour. She just said that there was no ham, but she could open a tin of pilchards, if I insisted.

Over tea I tried to explain that the Introduction posed rather a problem, as this book was a follow-up to a previous one.

'I've got to say the same things, but differently.'

'How differently?' Carrie demanded.

'Well, the book is mostly in verse, so I wondered if I could manage a verse Introduction.'

'Nobody uses verse for that sort of thing.'

I said that if Sir John Betjeman could write part of his autobiography in verse, there was no reason why I couldn't do an Introduction the same way. So I had started to have a go.

Lupin, our son, then came in, and after tea Carrie asked me to read what I had written so far. As it was in heroic couplets, I decided to stand on the table and declaim it:

' ''Twas ne'er the custom, not at any time
To introduce brief biographies in rhyme . . .
One hundred and fifty biographies, all of them potted
Crammed into the space oft to one allotted . . .'

8

At this point Lupin muttered: 'This is no good. It doesn't even scan. Unless it's meant to be a parody of McGonagall.'

I stepped forward to silence him, and fell off the table.

Wednesday

I woke this morning with an awful head. When I told Carrie, she said something about it looking the same as usual. When I scowled, she added: 'Don't you like your sort of jokes any more? Well, you can thank that silly verse of yours. You ought to know that no one writes rhymed poetry any more. Apart from Patience Strong, of course.'

Later, she brought me up my notebook, saying: 'Now you stick to prose if you know what's good for you.' But it wasn't as easy as that. By lunchtime I had got the following:

'The lives of folk of fame, in short, are here presented for us, for books of their lives are dearly bought and their great length would bore us. They tell of days oft bleak and grey, with thunder, rain and showers, or days when they were blithe and gay, 'midst many sunshine hours.'

When Lupin brought up my lunch, he glanced at my notebook while I ate one of Carrie's specialities, which she calls 'Fish Finger Surprise'.

'You can't use words like "gay",' he said.

'I have to. Nothing else rhymes.'

'That's the trouble with poetry,' growled Lupin. 'It's more concerned with form rather than inner truth. There's semolina shape.' Then he added with a rare touch of solicitude: 'I wouldn't, not if I was you.'

I went down for tea and Lupin surprised me by saying he had been pondering the problem of my Introduction.

'It's nice of you to take such an interest,' I said.

Carrie observed that they all wanted it out of the way so they could go back to living again.

'I read the other one you wrote for a book by these same people. *How to be Ridiculous* or some such.'

'*How to Become Ridiculously Well-Read in One Evening*,' I said, rather hurt.

'Well, you had a good introduction there. Said it all. How most literary encapsulations were boring, while yours are supposed to be funny. How shortened versions save people time and money, and how they cut down on shelf space in libraries, and save paper.

9

Well, why not say the same about a book of potted biographies? All the same stuff applies.'

I told him that was the problem – to find another way of saying the same thing.

'It applies even more for biographies,' said Lupin. 'They're longer. All those appendixes and scholarly footnotes.'

Carrie said they all contained too much about early struggles. 'One has enough of one's own without having to go through other people's as well. I don't know why you can't just say that nobody in their right minds would want to sit down and read over one hundred and sixty full-length biographies, even if they had the time left over from *Wogan* and *EastEnders*.' Carrie sounded weary.

'Not to mention sitting down and reading the same number of entries in a biographical dictionary,' observed Lupin. 'Not my idea of a jolly night's read. And talking of jolly evenings, where's my cap?'

'Have we helped?'

I nodded reluctantly. It's not the sort of admission I like to make to my own family. 'But I still have to structure it all, find a logical coherent way of putting it together. Something novel to engage the readers' attention.'

'You just put it down in a long piece, until you've said all you have to say, and then stop,' said Carrie.

'Unlike a lot of writers,' said Lupin, smarming his hair down in front of the mirror over the hearth. 'I suppose you could still go on with the idea of putting it into verse. Verse? Well, it's never been done before, I suppose.'

'At least once he's done it, no one will want to do it again,' said Carrie, and they both had another good laugh.

'What else have you got to get in?' asked Carrie, drying her eyes, after Lupin had gone.

'All about the contributors. How they are freelance writers who mostly do the various literary competitions, and how this whole book was a kind of literary competition, except that I revised and criticized all the submissions, and they were sometimes extensively re-written. In many cases, of course, I also suggested a treatment.'

'You could use T. S. Eliot, I suppose,' said Carrie. 'You have parodied him before, and he doesn't have to rhyme. Rhyme's difficult. I suppose that's the main cause of modern poetry.'

Later that evening I showed Carrie what I had written.

'A long competing they had of it
Almost the best part of a year
And such a year.
The papers coming and going so fast
That there were times when I regretted hearing the postman
Rejection was the cruellest decision.
Here I was, an old man on a new barge,
With no time to hear the wind
Singing in the rigging,
Even if there had been any rigging,
And always the demands for alterations,
Rewriting and partly rewriting.
Some of the famous were so popular
There were enough Spooners
To satisfy all the colleges of Oxford
And Lear was a King again.
At last we came to the book,
Whole, complete,
Of a length the publisher had demanded,
But in our end is our beginning.'

'I suppose that about sums it up,' said Carrie, when she had finished reading, 'though I can't understand the last line.'

'That's our next book, *The Dogsbody Papers*. It's what you might call a new look at history.'

'I've always thought history interesting. All that rape and war . . . and rape . . . incest . . . and so on.'

'They're writing it at the moment for publication next year. It will give you all the history you have never known before, though you ought to have done.'

Carrie sighed. 'I suppose you'll have the same trouble over the Introduction, only it'll be worse.'

'On the contrary, it'll be easier,' I said cheerfully. 'I shall get you and Lupin to write it again.'

E. O. PARROTT

HOW TO BECOME ABSURDLY WELL-INFORMED ABOUT THE FAMOUS AND INFAMOUS

SAPPHO (born *c.* mid 7th century BC)

'. . . *burning Sappho* . . .' (*Lord Byron*)

SAPPHO! A name that echoes down the ages . . .
    What was her secret, legendary poet?
May we inquire from history's dim pages
                        If they can show it?

Born in the Lesbian town of Mitylene,
    Author of hymns addressed to Aphrodite;
Some say her death was tragic (though a teeny
                        Little bit flighty):

Into the winds which wrack the rock Leucadia
    Leapt she, to land a wreck for waves to play on;
Love unrequited reached a fatal nadir
                        (*He* was called Phaon) . . .

As for all that, it seems to be a fiction;
    Still our attempts to learn the truth she parries.
Can we disclose some stowaway depiction
                        Which her *name* carries?

Did the SAP HOP in her when Spring was starting?
    Was it a PASH OP. that she was engaged in?
Sighed she, OH PAPS★! in ecstasy of parting
                        (★ What the heart's caged in)?

Not Cleopatra, who the ASP HOP greeted;
    Not Margareta, she in PA SHOP brought up,
(If she HAS POP, his name has been deleted)
                        But a girl caught up

Merely by love? 'PAH! SOP!' I hear you mutter,
    'Here's nothing strange, no shadowy enigma;
Have you no tale of darkling deeds to utter –
                        Sinister stigma?'

As for all *that*: the tales of orgies furnaced
    By heats unnatural – females gone berserk – 'll
Always be told, though facts suggest an earnest
                        Poetry Circle.

13

Can we insist the lady's not for burning
        (*Pace* Lord B.), that literary traffic's
All to be found that kept the Lesbians turning
                    Love into Sapphics?

Frankly, we can't; but, reader, do not blame us –
        Art has its truth, no seeker need forego it.
Who cares a damn for 'infamous' or 'famous'?
                    She was A POET.

                                MARY HOLTBY

PYTHAGORAS (582–500 BC)

Pythagoras was quite unfair on
        Boys and girls – but what's the use?
People *still* tell me there's a square on
        The hypotenuse.

Trust the hypotenuse; it's fine;
        It won't have snakes or bears on;
But nor, since it is just a line,
        Will it have squares on.

And yet when I said this at school,
        I had to spend my youth
In being called all sorts of fool
        For speaking truth.

Pythagoras, of Samian birth,
        Studied philosophy;
An ass, he thought, returned to earth
        As you or me.

Metempsychosis – transmigrating –
        Two frightful words to spell;
A frightful notion also, rating
        A padded cell.

Yet to this madman's tender cares
        They gave my adolescence,
Commanding to his silly squares
        My acquiescence.

14

His followers were set on fire
  Around five ten B.C.,
A date in history to inspire
  The likes of me.

My teachers' lives have terminated;
  So has Pythagoras's;
In case they've all been transmigrated
  I'm kind to asses.

PAUL GRIFFIN

...agoras, Greek mystic, sage
...nd scholar of the golden age,
Was to doubt and schism prone
So he launched out on his own,
Teaching at his new foundation,
Of the soul and transmigration,
How material wealth demeans,
And why no one should eat beans.
Just such notions, only cornier,
Are still found in California.

Lest I hear you mutter
He was just a nutter,
Let me set you right,
He deserved his fame:
At the numbers game
He was out of sight.

Suppose we have a triangle with three
Vertices labelled 'A' and 'B' and 'C',
Also suppose one corner, such as A
Is right-angled exactly, then we say
The side BC which faces A is known
As the Hypotenuse. It is then shown
That if upon that side we put a square
And put two on the others to compare,
The total area on the other two's
The same as that on the hypotenuse.
This theorem Pythagoras begot,
And also proved, which I, alas, cannot.

NOEL PETTY

CONFUCIUS (Latinized form of K'UNG FU-TSE) (551–479 BC)

As the white cherry blossoms drift down
Upon the snowy head of the revered sage,
At his feet still the disciples listen
To the words of wisdom that fall from his lips.
They drift down among them like snowflakes
In the silence by the fountain.
Is he thinking of those early years of poverty
After his father was killed in the wars,
Or the moment when as a young man
He dedicated himself to learning?
He knows that his years as a major
And minister in the province of Lu,
Reforming the laws and building drains,
Won him the praise and the enmity of neighbouring dukes,
So that he was forced to go upon his wanderings.
Although Lu finally received him with honour again,
He was now too wise to be a minister.
As the musician fingers the strings of his instrument,
The philosopher may recall that it was he
Who found new ways to sing the odes of old.
And still the blossoms fall
As the sage gives voice to his wise sayings,
And the disciples listen in reverence.
But his children prefer to watch the cherry blossoms;
They have heard all his sayings many times.
The daily repetition of these moral maxims
Makes them think it is like
Having a calendar for a father.
Even the cherry blossom trusts that it is falling
Into an oblivion where there are no more
Tedious platitudes of an old man mumbling into his beard.

E. O. PARROTT

AESCHYLUS (525–456 BC)

A fragment of a lost play, The Poets

[*A* MESSENGER *enters and sees a lock of hair.*]

MESSENGER: Ah! But see – his hair, tied lock-wise!

CHORUS OF
ATHENIANS: Who? Say who once wore this hair piece?

MESSENGER: Old and dry, how long past growing!

ATHENIANS: Old it is but who once wore it?

MESSENGER: This did once adorn a poet.
Can I bring myself to say it,
Knowing how my news brings sadness?

ATHENIANS: Tell us first whose hair this once was;
Then relate your fateful tidings.

MESSENGER: Aeschylus, dramatic poet . . .

ATHENIANS: Can it be that this was his?

MESSENGER: Loved of all the men of Athens,
His this ancient lock of hair is,
He the subject of my tidings!
When he fought beside our fathers –
Standing firm, those men of Athens –
At Marathon and then Salamis,
How his locks, well-oiled and waving
Flashed and shone in heat of battle!
In peace began his feats of writing,
And so began the steady balding.
Each festive play in competition
Brought him honour, fame and moulting.
As the years passed so his hair fell,
One by one the strands descending,
Floating grave and white to earthward.
Each play defeated by the young ones,
Sophocles, the young pretender,
Brought another sorry thatch-fall!

ATHENIANS: This we know. Now give your message!

MESSENGER: Standing baldly under heaven,
Rock-like seemed his noble skull-top.
Then soared an eagle, ever upwards,
On Aeschylus his eye remaining,
A tortoise in his firm claw clasping.
With steady wing and aim unswerving,
The noble bird released the tortoise,

Like a thunderbolt fast-falling
On the guiltless poet's skull-top.
Tears fill my eyes at my recalling
The head that sired so many dramas
Defeated by a plunging tortoise!
[*The* ATHENIANS *utter strange cries and begin to
    dance* . . .]

N. J. WARBURTON

SOCRATES (469–399 BC)

Young Socrates, an ugly youth –
No one could ever call him couth –
May have been an Attic hippy
When he shacked up with Xanthippe.
(One wonders how, when he was older,
He coped with such a frightful scolder.)
But later on he came to reach a
Ripe maturity as teacher.
Helped by his 'daemon', he began
Examining the moral man.
'The only thing with power to hurt you
Is ignorance,' he taught, 'and virtue
Issues from acquiring knowledge.'
The public places were his College,
And there, to questions subtly wise,
His pupils found their own replies.
This sort of thing, of course, did not
Please the higher-ups a lot.
Athenian authorities
Had different priorities.
They said his lack of piety
Corrupted young society.
And, jealous of each shibboleth,
They sentenced Socrates to death.
He spent his last days with his friends
Who tidied up his life's loose ends,
And then he took the hemlock cup
And calmly drank the whole thing up.

JOYCE JOHNSON

18

PLATO (428–348 BC)

You to whom the term 'Platonic'
    Simply signifies 'unsexy',
    Dons, just short of apoplexy,
Would dismiss in tones sardonic.
Far from concepts so moronic,
    They debate (diverse, emphatic)
    How much Plato is Socratic?
How much Socrates Platonic?

We will not presume to traffic
    In such learned, analytic
    Intricacies of the critic,
Since our aim is biographic:
Athens was his native city,
    Socrates his favoured master,
    In whose death, he shows us, passed a
Man of virtue, wise and witty.

Plato travelled widely, leaving
    Murderous Athens far behind him,
    Till in Sicily we find him
At the tyrant's court, receiving
Friendship from his kinsman, Dion;
    Formed in Athens on returning
    An Academy of learning,
Such as all men might rely on.

Since the aim of all his teaching
    Was for Wisdom's cause to flourish,
    Fervently he longed to nourish
Rulers in that art – and reaching
For the opening afforded,
    Went to Syracuse again; he reckoned
    Dionysius the Second
Might be trained, and he rewarded.

Philosophic constitution
    Couldn't be achieved by Plato;
    Found the heir a hot potato,
Baked in self-esteem's pollution.

Undervalued, unregarded,
    Wisdom in the streets goes crying;
    So the king, her grace denying,
Acts no better than his pa did.

Plato's back to theorizing . . .
    In his books appear dramatic
    Presentations of Socratic
Notions (as, from early prizing
Passions individualistic,
    Man may rise above the bestial
    To perceive the pure, celestial
Beauty cherished by the mystic).

Did the elder sage his cub lick
    Into shape – his own – or was it
    Progress from a firm deposit
Formed of *Phaedo*, *Laws*, *Republic*,
And the rest, a *Feast* symphonic?
    Cookery is never static:
    Let jingredients be Socratic,
But proclaim the chef Platonic.

MARY HOLTBY

ARISTOTLE (384–322 BC)

Aristotle is a name
Great in academic fame:
Born in BC 384
Far on Halkidiki's shore,
Plato's pupil, fine disputer,
Mighty Alexander's tutor,
Taught his followers Aesthetics,
Politics, Apologetics,
Rhetoric, Empiricism,
Physics, and the Syllogism,
Wrote on these, and on Poetics,
Works that make good anaesthetics
For the likes of you and me
Who can grasp one word in three.

Students driven to the bottle
By the works of Aristotle
Think it justice beyond question
That he died of indigestion.

PAUL GRIFFIN

EUCLID (*c*. 300 BC)

PROPOSITION:
Euclid was a Greek mathematician who taught in Alexandria about
300 BC, and whose principal work *The Elements* first put
mathematics on a logical foundation.

PROOF:
Hypothesis: Let us suppose that the proposition is false. Let us
suppose, in fact, that Euclid was a travelling dry goods salesman
working out of South Bend, Indiana, who liked fudge brownies,
supported the Brooklyn Dodgers, and did a little fishing in the
creek on weekends.

Then his sales territory would be within two hundred miles of
South Bend, Indiana.

But Chicago, home of the Chicago White Sox, is less than two
hundred miles from South Bend, Indiana.

Axiom: No storekeeper within five hundred miles of Chicago
would buy his dry goods supplies from a supporter of the Brooklyn
Dodgers.

Therefore no storekeeper in Euclid's territory would buy his dry
goods supplies from Euclid.

Therefore Euclid never made a sale.

Therefore Euclid was not a travelling dry goods salesman.

Which contradicts the hypothesis.

Wherefore the original proposition is correct. Q.E.D.

NOEL PETTY

ARCHIMEDES (287–212 BC)

'You stink!' cried Archimedes' spouse.
'Your odour permeates the house.
Go give yourself a thorough scrub.'
So Archimedes took his tub;
Then, suddenly, with whoops of glee
About his body's buoyancy,
He upped and ran through Syracuse,
Still naked, and gave out his news:
'Eureka, folks! I can relate
Water displacement to lost weight.'
At home he told his scolding wife:
'This is the triumph of my life.
You said I reeked; I say: "Eureka!"
(It's more exciting and much Greeker).
Let's drink a celebratory cup
Because my Principle stands up.'
'Well, that's a change,' his consort said.
'Lately it's been a flop in bed.'
'Peace, woman!' snapped the angry sage.
'Stop talking sex and act your age.'
(This from the great inventor who
Was working on the Endless Screw!)
When Archimedes, growing old,
Was drawing plans in sand, we're told;
A Roman military lout
Callously stamped his sketches out.
The sage protested, but in vain,
And on the spot was cruelly slain.
One must deplore his mindless slaughter –
This man of weighty thoughts on water.

PETER VEALE

HOMER (?–? BC)

Homer nods . . .

Homer was a noddy, see?
Didn't write the Odyssey,

22

Didn't write the Iliad;
Wasn't blind, and didn't sing
Epics to the local king . . .

Not a woman, I might add,
Though I grant the term 'Misnomer'
Obviously applies to Homer.

MARY HOLTBY

HANNIBAL (247–182 BC)

He'll be coming down the mountain when he comes
In the bitter wind that batters and benumbs;
He'll be coming down the mountain and I see the vultures counting,
They'll be counting up the corpses as he comes.

He was born a Carthaginian, and his Dad
Was anxious to indoctrinate the lad
So he took him into battle and informed his offspring: 'That'll
Show you something of the hassle that we've had.

Here's an altar, and before I let you go,
You must swear undying hatred to the foe!'
So for all the Roman nation he declared his detestation,
Which in later life he had a chance to show:

Fought bravely under Hasdrubal in Spain
And himself at last conducted the campaign.
To restore some sort of order Rome set Ebro as a border,
For a peaceable division of terrain;

But Saguntum, on the Carthaginian side,
The Romans in their arrogance denied.
This Hannibal found shocking, so he gave the town a knocking
And began to plan his celebrated ride.

For the Romans had declared the Punic War,
And Hannibal remembered what he swore.
'Now that Rome has tried to burke us we shall treat her to a circus
Of a kind she's not experienced before.'

So he settles on the Alps for his Big Top,
Where the elephants go dancing till they drop;
At sour wine his clowns may grumble but it makes the rockface
    crumble
And in Italy the hissing has to stop.

He beat Scipio, the first upon the scene;
Lured Flaminius to his fate at Trasimene;
And at Cannae (somewhat later, thanks to Fabius Cunctator)
Threw a spanner in the Roman war machine.

But alas! this was the highlight of the show;
His country is in trouble – he must go,
And the end of all the drama is the battlefield of Zama,
Where he can't escape the scourge of Scipio.

Defeated, he still rules his native state,
But the Romans want his blood and will not wait;
He flees, and raises forces, but exhausting his resources
He eventually fixes his own fate.

Though for cruelty the Romans curse his name
And palpitating pachyderms may claim
That they hold the same opinion, this ingenious Carthaginian
Was a hero who deserves immortal fame.

MARY HOLTBY

CLEOPATRA (68–30 BC)

Here Cleopatra lies – O wail,
    You leaders of society!
And let the moral of my tale
    Recall you to propriety;
The dreadful consequences gauge
Of envying a queen whose age
Can't wither her (nor custom stale
    Her infinite variety).

Though booked as heir to Egypt's throne
    And bride to brother Ptolemy,
Some thought he ought to rule alone
    And set a corps to collar me.

Expelled unwillingly to Spain,
Great Caesar brought me back again,
Proclaimed the kingdom as my own
    And made a gangster's moll o' me.

Now brotherless, I ruled at home,
    And bore a boy, Caesarion;
Then followed Caesar back to Rome . . .
    A brutish libertarian
Contrived to bring about his fate
And stabbed him on that very date
Which some soothsaying astronome
    Had warned him to be wary on.

To Egypt I returned as queen,
    And there arrived Antonius;
Soon as he came upon the scene
    Relations were harmonious.
In fact we had a lot of fun
For years, till Actium was won –
Where my activities had been,
    Said angry Ant, felonious.

News of my death could hardly fail
    To soothe him to sobriety;
He slew himself when told the tale,
    So, feeling some anxiety
Lest Rome my final shame should stage,
I took an asp, and that's why age
Can't wither me, and playwrights hail
    My infinite variety.

MARY HOLTBY

BOADICEA (?–AD 61)

She grew up to be queen of Iceni,
The original babe in the woad;
The king wasn't known as a meanie
In Norfolk, his normal abode.

For Prasutagus – that was his name –
Had submitted to Claudian virtue:
That is, you play Rome at its game,
And its legions are sure not to hurt you.

But alas, when young Nero succeeded,
And Prasutagus dropped in his tracks,
His arrangements went largely unheeded,
And the Latin lot packed up the *pax*.

Prasutagus' wife, Boadicea,
And his two noble daughters, protested –
The Iceni had always been free-er,
Why now were their people molested?

They flogged her, and raped both her daughters,
Which didn't appeal to the regions.
She rallied the tribes from all quarters,
To slaughter the alien legions.

The Iceni were armed to the teeth;
They had scythes on their chariot wheels;
Were Romans near home, hearth or heath,
Boadicea was hot on their heels.

She fell upon Colchester, furious,
She ordered an orgy of gore,
And she led, since you're obviously curious,
A cool quarter-million or more.

She lynched and she lashed and she ravaged,
She struck with the sword and with fire;
With London and Verulam savaged,
She watched the Ninth Legion expire.

It fell to Suetonius Paulinus
(Away on a mission in Wales)
To return to the scene of such heinous
Revenges – beyond any pales.

Boadicea, with wagons and horses,
Found the Romans with woods all around,
But while she was sorting her forces,
She was charged on the very same ground.

The Iceni were reckless, unready,
And were hacked down, their kids by their side.
Boadicea, her nerve now unsteady,
Took poison, and drank it, and died.

Now Norfolk has resident yokels
Who live at a pacified pace:
But say 'Boadicea', and locals
Will cheer till they're blue in the face!

BILL GREENWELL

CALIGULA (Gaius Caesar Augustus Germanicus) (12–41)

Social worker's report

I have made several visits to the home of Mr Gaius and, although
he refused to co-operate in the intelligence and psychological tests
I attempted to administer, I feel I have seen enough to make
certain recommendations. Mr Gaius is, in many ways, a personable
young man and shows all the signs of having been brought up in a
very good family. His father, Mr Germanicus, was an army officer,
much respected and with a considerable reputation which my client
may have found rather daunting. I am certain that the death of Mr
Germanicus while his son was still impressionable has much to do
with the delinquency with which we are now faced. Mr Gaius has
a well-appointed home in the best part of Rome and is, at the
moment, holding down an extremely demanding and responsible
job. He is a devoted family man and my conversations with his
sisters have revealed that he is able to show them great affection.
This, surely, must stand in his favour. He is also fond of animals
and has made his horse a member of the Senate. Many of his
problems stem from the fact that he considers himself to be divine.
This has meant that he is unusually resistant to suggestions that he
should join self-help groups or undertake courses of behavioural
therapy.

Recommendations: Mr Gaius needs careful handling and at
this stage of his development concerned parties should go along
with the view that he is a god. A small team of support social
workers should make regular visits in order to monitor progress

and to worship him. This should help him to build a healthy self-image. In the meantime, I suggest that his file be classified 'strictly confidential' and passed on to the Praetorian Guard.

N. J. WARBURTON

NERO CLAUDIUS CAESAR (37–68)

The emperor Nero from his youth
Was quite remarkably uncouth.
Of Claudius the adopted son,
He soon dispatched the natural one,
Although already named the heir,
Thanks to his mother's thoughtful care.
(In time her bossy manner grated;
He had the hag assassinated.)
He made Octavia his wife;
Divorced her first, then took her life.
Between the two he wed Poppaea,
Whose junketings would cost her dear –
For in a pet he aimed a kick
Which struck her dead who once was quick.
These incidents might well suffice
To prove he wasn't very nice;
Strangely, the crime well known to you
Was one he didn't really do –
The fire that found him on the fiddle
Presents, it seems, an unsolved riddle.
He blamed the Christians, gaining thence
A lot of fun at their expense.
As things grew worse a certain Piso
Decided that this needn't be so;
It didn't take our hero long
To prove him and his comrades wrong,
Nor, with the rest, to execute a
Poor guiltless man, his former tutor,
The playwright, Seneca (who boasts
A corpus full of blood and ghosts).
Into the marital arena
Came post-Poppaean Messalina;

28

She managed to outlive her mate,
Who met a self-inflicted fate:
On learning he was on the shelf
And Galba reigned, he stabbed himself.
     The life of Nero seems to me
A study in tautology.
It's fair enough to pogrom preachers,
But rivals, mothers, wives, *and* teachers,
Piled high upon the bloodstained flooring
End up as desperately boring.

MARY HOLTBY

LADY GODIVA (?–1080)

The Parable of the Naked Lady

1. And it came to pass in the reign of King Canute that Leofric, Earl of Mercia, laid a heavy burden of tax upon the people that dwelt in the city of Coventry.

2. For Leofric was taken with wickedness and did persecute both church and people.

3. And Leofric had a wife who was called Godiva and she was sore troubled by the plight of the people.

4. And Godiva spake unto Leofric saying: Husband, why treat you so the people? And she beseeched him to lift the tax from the people.

5. And Leofric replied unto her saying: If your love for the people be so great, cast off thy raiment and let your nakedness be the sign of your devotion. Then will I ease the people's burden.

6. For Leofric knew in his heart that the piety of his wife would not allow such a thing to come to pass.

7. Then straightway did Godiva cast off her raiment, yea, verily unto the very last stitch, and did mount an ass with only the hairs of her head for a cloak.

8. Thus did she journey the highways of Coventry.

9. And the multitude hid their eyes from her and did not look upon the nakedness of the woman or her ass.

10. Save for one whose name was Thomas. And Thomas looked upon the woman in her nakedness and did tremble about the loins.

11. And the Lord said: As ye peepeth so shall ye reapeth. And the sight of Thomas was taken away even unto the end of his days.

12. And Leofric was amazed at that which had come to pass and he repented and lifted the yoke of taxes which was upon the people saying: Wife, your nakedness has turned my heart.

13. Then in union did Leofric and Godiva build an holy place for prayer and contemplation.

14. And when Godiva was grown old and her breath was taken away, then was she laid to rest in that place and her husband before her.

V. ERNEST COX

WILLIAM I (1027–87)

William the Conqueror

'Crumbs! Me, King of England!' exclaimed William. 'Cor!'

'You gotter invade!' insisted 'Ginger' Odo. 'Ol' Ted promised you'd have that there crown.'

'If I don't become Queen,' cried Matilda Elizabeth, 'I shall thcweam and thcweam and thcweam until I'm thick. I tan, you know.'

'You get on wiv your rotten ol' tap'stry,' said Henri, being as helpful as he felt a squire ought to be.

'That there 'Arold said he'd back me for King,' said William angrily. 'Now that Ted has snuffed it, he's took it hisself.'

'William, if you don't spifflicate Harold,' said Matilda Elizabeth, 'I shall thcweam and . . .'

'Orl right, orl right,' said William hastily, 'I'm goin'. I'll shoot an arrer into his eye. Or somethink . . . Where shall we land, Ginger?'

'Hastings. It's handy. 'Sides, the pier's nicer.'

'I 'spect I'll make you a bishop, or somethink, for helpin' me, Ginger.'

'I'm not religious.'

'You don't have to be religious to be a bishop. Not today,' Douglas pointed out.

''Sides,' said Ginger, 'I'm a bishop already. Of Bay Oh, or somewhere.'

'We'd better get on with the invasion,' said William, 'or it'll be time to go home for tea. It's a bastard, having bin Duke of Normandy for so long.'

'It was bein' a bastard made you Duke,' said Douglas.

'When you're king, William,' said Matilda, 'you can take all the land.'

'And have huntin' forests where you can chase boars!' said Ginger, excitedly.

'You mean like Robert?' William asked.

'Boars are animals, stupid!' said Matilda Elizabeth. 'But they get made 'stinct, I 'spect.'

'I 'spect they stinked all the time,' said Henri, but the others didn't hear him. They were busy looking at a large book.

'I shall write down all the houses and animals and things in England and who owns them,' said William, 'and then tell 'em I own it all.'

'It stands to reason,' said 'Ginger' Odo. 'If you're King, it's all yours. That's the feudal system, 'cos you feud wiv everyone.'

'How long are you going to be King for?' asked Henri, who was beginning to get tired of being a mere squire.

'I 'spect until I'm really very, very old. Like thirty-seven. Or sixty, mebbe. Yes, sixty will do, and then I'll be killed in a war or somethink. Come on. It's time for tea.'

E. O. PARROTT

MATILDA (1102–67)

Do you remember your reign, Matilda?
    Do you remember your reign?
When your poor old Dad
All those lampreys had,
And you came back again
To claim as your own the English throne,
Which your cousin Stephen
Was bold enough even
To decry and defy
And even deny.
Do you remember your reign, Matilda?
    Do you remember your reign?

When cousin fought cousin
Causing a dozen
Years' struggle that killed a
Lot who were not
Concerned in the plot,
And every bod
Then said that God
And his angels slept,
And widows wept,
And all was in vain.
Do you remember your reign, Matilda?
    Do you remember your reign?

How you endured
Being immured
In that castle at Oxon,
The gates with the locks on,
The empty larder,
And life getting harder,
The grope for the rope in the sudden hope
Of escape, and the scrape
Of the hand-under-hand,
Till you came down to land
In the soft silent snow.
It was touch-and-go.
And the flight, dight in white,
As you and your men,
As you and four men
Went silent as mices over the Isis,
Now frozen deep.
Were the guards asleep?
Do you remember that night, Matilda?
    Do you remember that night?

Nevermore, Matilda, nevermore
Were things as before.
You were shown the door
By Stephen, for
You had to admit it was high time to quit it.
It was just too bad,
And rather sad,
For as England's Queen you might have been
So very much more.

JOYCE JOHNSON

ST THOMAS
(THOMAS À BECKET) (1118–70)

When April showers bring on the Spring
And wakeful birds are stirred to sing,
You might expect the youth to yearn;
If so, you've something else to learn.
It seems that folk in former ages
Felt moved to go on pilgrimages;
The cured were least inclined to duck it;
Their goal – where Becket kicked the bucket.
His shrine brought spiritual profit
(And Canterbury prospered off it).
    But medieval thaumaturges
Are prone, like us, to natural urges,
Though these, it seems, in Thomas' case,
Were less to lust than pride of place.
French-trained in law, and then installed
Aide to Archbishop Theobald,
Who made him, though in minor orders,
His spy on clerical marauders,
He caught King Henry's notice, and
Became chief lawyer of the land.
Chuffed Chancellor and monarch wily
Together led the life of Riley,
Till, basking in this genial climate,
The hapless Henry made him Primate.
In cope and mitre smartly dressed,
He now assumes a scratchy vest,
Resigns his former job, supports
The Church's office in the courts:
A change of front to suit his calling
Which Henry found extremely galling.
They quarrelled on from year to year
(Fresh grounds were punctual to appear),
Till exiled Tom defied his master,
And made for Dover and disaster
(Though hearing of a hostile band which
Awaited him, changed course for Sandwich).
    'Who'll rid me of this meddling priest?'
You'll recognize these words at least,
Unwisely by the King employed

33

When understandably annoyed.
Four barons were prepared to judge
This outburst as a royal nudge,
And left for Canterbury, where
They put an end to the affair . . .
Or so they thought – but those who barter
A live Archbishop for a martyr
May find themselves miscalculating,
To ill effect, their audience rating.
    The King was shattered by remorse
And screamed and cried till he was hoarse,
And where the martyr's blood had dripped
He had himself severely whipped.
Then, since on evidence empirical –
An outbreak of attested miracle –
The prelate's sainthood was displayed,
Such he officially was made.
The richest shrine that could be built
Was Henry's penance for his guilt,
And there the eager pilgrims throng
When April bursts in shower and song.

MARY HOLTBY

ROBIN HOOD (12th–13th century)

From a lost novel by D. H. Lawrence

He loved the Midlands – this green, rolling, throbbing heart of
England. Whose England, though? The old England of the
Lionheart, who had ruled by his natural, inalienable male
authority? Or the wretched new England of that snivelling, devious
usurper, Prince John? In a queer way these unnatural brothers
reminded him of his own two selves. His former life as Robert
Fitzooth, Earl of Huntingdon, he now despised utterly. Now, as
the outlaw Robin Hood, he was a lord of life; he knew deep in his
solar plexus that the Lincoln green mantle he wore, the cock
pheasant's plume that sprouted from his jutting cap, the taut
longbow slung across his back, were his by right. His merry men
acknowledged him as their leader by sheer force of his will; the
urgent tug of his tumescent blood drew them to serve him
unquestioningly, blindly.

    He began to skin the powerful stag that had, a few minutes

earlier, blundering through the undergrowth, been checked by a single, unerring arrow from his bulging quiver. What if the law said this was royal venison? He knew that, by the laws of nature, this was his meat, won in equal combat between man and beast. He had felt a mutual respect, even a queer kind of love, flowing between him and this great, muscular stag in those ecstatic seconds before he released his dark seed of destruction.

His deft, almost feminine fingers paused as he heard his fellow-outlaws approaching, and he looked up, smiling almost shyly in the flush of his success. At their head was Little John, the most virile, upstanding member of his band, walking with his proud head erect. Behind came the others, their heads bowed in humble obeisance to Robin's unflinching will. Bringing up the rear – how gracefully, how appropriately she did so! – was Lady Marion, the noblewoman who had thrown in her lot with him, sworn to obey every manly whim of this queer green man whose pagan male authority dragged at her loins with an unquenchable magnetism.

PETER NORMAN

FRANCESCO PETRARCA
(Petrarch) (1304–74)

Petrarca, though he was Italian-born,
Grew up in the entourage of the Pope,
Who had, when things got hot, abandoned hope
And made a home from Rome in Avignon.
'Twas there Petrarca (though not *sur le pont*)
First saw his Laura. He began to mope
With unrequited love, which gave him scope
For verses touching those whom love has lorn.
He knew his constancy would never vary
Though separation was to be his fate.
His lyric genius was legendary,
And Rome (most aptly) crowned him *Laureate*.
The songs and sonnets, called the *Canzoniere*,
First scanned the compass of the human state.

Whether Petrarca first performed the feat
Of rhyming sonnets in this special way
I'm not quite sure, but be that as it may,
It's called Petrarcan, and it's pretty neat:

35

You rhyme A-B-B-A, and then repeat
Another just the same, A-B-B-A,
And having done this first eight-line array,
The section called the octave is complete.
A pause for breath at this stage is decreed –
Enjambement is considered rather poor –
For now we're in the sestet part, you see,
And so to wrap it up you merely need
A C-D-E, then C-D-E once more,
Or possibly C-D-C-D-C-D.

NOEL PETTY

TAMBURLAINE (1336–1405)

Great Tamburlaine, who ruled with fire and sword,
Was, in effect, a one-man Mongol horde.
On various of his numerous excursions
He slaughtered loads of Mamelukes and Persians,
But after he'd disposed of Asia Minor,
He couldn't find much left to sack but China.
He thus took steppes to execute this plan,
But soon, now nearing man's allotted span,
And past retirement age for rape and pillage,
Died with his boots off in some Kazakh village.
He is remembered for his roaring rages;
Also for keeping conquered kings in cages.

NOEL PETTY

GEOFFREY CHAUCER (c. 1340–1400)

Geoffrey Chaucer, to speke trewe,
Was sad and thinne and pale of hewe.
His fader in London kepte his home,
Selling wyn to alle and some –
The Kynge himselfë boghte of it.
This Geoffrey was a manne of wyt

And verray mobile uppëwarde,
Served Kynge Edward as a garde
And as a Civil Servant eke
In postës nombreless to speke.
Poemes of many kyndes he maad,
Of Troilus and his Criseyde,
Of Halwed Ladies, Fowlës, Fame,
And yaf himselfe a noble name.
Allas, he spente and took no care
As monie out of fashioun were,
And ever as a bombe he maad
In debte he wente, and so he staied.
So attë laste, and fer fro murie
He toke his horse to Canterburie
And tho his Tales gan to write
In which his genie shineth brighte.
Some Tales are coarse, and some are coarser.
I have namore to seyn of Chaucer.

PAUL GRIFFIN

WAT TYLER (?-1381)

A man ther was, a TYLER for the nones;
That he was colerik he maad no bones.
Wel loved he to rumble and to rippe,
And on his shoulders bar he many a chippe.
Walter he highte, and as the tale ranne
From Inland Revenuë cam a manne
Who attë Walter's doghter maad a passe,
The which discomforted the vertuous lasse.
This Walter (Wat, as many did hym calle)
Lette out his braynës onnës and for alle.

So grete a smertë was fro this evente,
The peple roose in Essex and in Kente,
And with Jack Straw a ryot was begonne
(The yeere, iwis, was 1381).
To Maidstone rannë peple one and alle
And fro prisoun released they John Ball.

Withouten staie to Temple Barre yshope
They slawe of Caunterbury Archbishope;
Thennes to Smithfield, wher the yongë kynge,
The second Richard, heeld them parleyinge.
With othës grete our Walter shente him soore,
Til London's Mayor colde endure namoore;
Anon he strookë Wat; what maie I seye?
For fro his brest the soulë paste awaie.

   The yongë kynge, he laughed like a drayne
And seyde: 'Frend, this Tyler was a peyne.
Wel hastow don to sleyn hym with an axe,
For deed be hym who wol nat paie hire taxe!'

   And thennesforth, as ilke wight maie wist,
The Inland Revenue doon as they list.
They tak our tittle and they tak our jot;
And it is don in memorie of Wat.

PAUL GRIFFIN

TOMÁS DE TORQUEMADA (1420–98)

Torquemada: Spanish prelate,
Grand Inquisitor and zealot.
Expert on the bastinado,
Thumbscrew, iron boot, strappado,
Freezing, burning, flagellation.
Racking, flaying, lapidation,
Iron maidens, leather muzzles,
Branding irons and crossword puzzles.

NOEL PETTY

WILLIAM CAXTON (1422–91)

A man yclept Will Caxton I must mencion,
Who brought to Engeland a new invencion,
And I woude say, *sans* ballyhoo or hype,
He was a verray parfit gentil type.
At Westminster he putte his printing presse,
And made a goodlie fortune, I woude gesse:

A scoler, eke, of many tongues, also,
He render'd into English Cicero,
And divers saucie tales he got from France,
Which made the Prioresse look askance.
He brought a litel John Bulle printing sette,
With all the letters of the alphabette,
And every morn the pilgrims he woude grete,
And give them all a newlie printed shete,
To read ere they began their dailie stint,
'Twas headed: 'All the News That's Fit to Print'.
He was ambicious, and brook'd no stopping,
Quod he: 'I'll ope another presse at Wapping'.
And by the holy martir he woude swear
That in tyme he'd become a millionaire.

                              STANLEY J. SHARPLESS

CHRISTOPHER COLUMBUS (1451–1506)

Christopher Columbus –
    What did he do?
He made of world geography
    A pain for me and you;
A chap who, born in *Genoa*,
    Leaves *Lisbon* for the Main,
Trades round the coast of *Africa*,
    Then rushes off to *Spain* . . .

Christopher Columbus –
    What was his quest?
To find a passage to the *East*
    Proceeding by the *West*.
To him *Bahamas* were *Chinese*
    (No doubt for reasons weighty);
Hispaniola, if you please,
    Was what he christened *Haiti*.

Christopher Columbus –
    What did he see?
He toured the *Caribbean*, and
    He saw the '*Indian*' Sea.

39

For *Asia* he found *Trinidad*
    (His sailors thought him *loco*)
But what a lovely time he had
    Around the *Orinoco*!

Christopher Columbus –
    A worthy work began
(*Honduras*, yes, and *Panama*,
    When looking for *Japan*)
And if he got his colleagues' goat,
    He likewise drives us frantic,
Who can't see why *West Indies* float
    Serene in the *Atlantic* . . .

MARY HOLTBY

LEONARDO DA VINCI (1452–1519)

OFFICIAL: So, you wish to apply for a . . . er . . .

LEONARDO: An Arts Council Grant. That's right.

OFFICIAL: Well, I'm sure you appreciate that competition is stiff and we have to be sure our money is well spent.

LEONARDO: Oh yes. I think I can safely say my interests are wide-ranging. Let me see. Yes, I almost discovered the circulation of the blood.

OFFICIAL: Almost?

LEONARDO: Yes. Tricky stuff, blood, you know. What else? Er . . . there were the aeroplanes . . .

OFFICIAL: Sorry? The what?

LEONARDO: Aeroplanes. They're sort of machines. That fly.

OFFICIAL: Good lord!

LEONARDO: Only they didn't quite get off the ground, so to speak.

OFFICIAL: I see.

LEONARDO: Then there was the submarine.

OFFICIAL: And did that get off the ground?

LEONARDO: [*Laughing*] I should think not. It was a machine for going under water . . .

OFFICIAL: Under?

LEONARDO: Yes.

OFFICIAL: And you could show us one?

LEONARDO: Not as such. It's still at what you might call the concept stage.

OFFICIAL: This is all very interesting, Mr Vincent . . .

LEONARDO: Da Vinci.

OFFICIAL: . . . and forgive me if this sounds Philistine but we are an *Arts* Council and you are sounding increasingly like an engineer so . . .

LEONARDO: I paint as well.

OFFICIAL: Ah!

LEONARDO: And sculpt.

OFFICIAL: Go on.

LEONARDO: For instance, there was the equestrian monument to Francesco Sforza. Ever come across it?

OFFICIAL: Public monument? Bronze?

LEONARDO: Fairly public, yes. Not quite bronze, I must admit.

OFFICIAL: What then?

LEONARDO: Clay.

OFFICIAL: Clay? I'm no sculptor, Mr Davidson . . .

LEONARDO: Da Vinci.

OFFICIAL: . . . but doesn't clay *sag* a bit when exposed to the elements?

LEONARDO: It was meant to end up as bronze but . . .

OFFICIAL: . . . You didn't quite finish it.

LEONARDO: Not the bronze version, no. I've been working on another one, though. For the king of France.

OFFICIAL: And this is clay too, is it?

LEONARDO: Not quite. At the moment it's mostly sketches and things.

OFFICIAL: [*Making notes*] Tell me about the paintings.

LEONARDO: Right. There's 'The Last Supper'. That was a biggie.

OFFICIAL: Finished?

LEONARDO: Yes. [*Slight pause.*] More or less.

OFFICIAL: Enough for us to see?

LEONARDO: Ah. Well, I'm afraid I made a bit of a cock-up with the medium on that one. Oil on plaster. Doesn't really go, you know.

OFFICIAL: Yes, well . . .

LEONARDO: [*Hurriedly*] And 'The Battle of Anghiari'. Another wall job. Plenty of action: horses, fighting, that kind of thing.

OFFICIAL: Complete?

LEONARDO: Oh yes.

OFFICIAL: Yes?

LEONARDO: Well, some of it is. I would've done the lot but there was this other bloke working on the opposite wall. Michelangelo. Absolute swine. Dabbing away and muttering to himself all day . . .

OFFICIAL: Be that as it may, Mr Leonard, we haven't got an awful lot to go on, have we? It may seem stuffy of us, but we do tend to go for things that are, well, carried through. They don't have to be good but we do like them finished.

LEONARDO: [*Desperately*] I've done a treatise on painting.

OFFICIAL: Published?

LEONARDO: In note form at the moment.

OFFICIAL: Look, have you thought about designing Christmas cards? Small scale, perhaps, but it would give you the chance to see something through. Take my advice: start in January, then come and see us again in a year. O.K.?

N. J. WARBURTON

MICHELANGELO (1475–1564)

Michelangelo,
in fourteen seventy-five,
was diminutive.
　　'Where am I?' he cried,
　　and was told: 'It's Florence, love –
　　just another shove . . .
It's fun being born.'
Thus, the wee rapscallion,
was Italian.
　　From an early age,
　　like all Florentines, a wit,
　　he drew on Mum's tit,
progressing to paint,
etch, sketch, carve in stone and wood,
whatever he could;
　　such precocity,
　　that before he had shaved,
　　Mike had done David.
His mates went beserk.
'*Viva Buonarroti!*':

42

Florence . . . quite dotty.
   Marbles and bronzes,
   pietàs of all sizes,
   other surprises,
until Julius
said: 'I pray this young chap'll
paint the Sistine Chapel',
   which he did, supine.
   Paul the Third was impressed;
   felt the work blessed.
Apart from these popes,
Cosimo de' Medici,
thought his stuff 'peachy'.
   In Rome, he drank with
   Giorgio Vasari,
   the odd Campari.
Myopic matrons,
now frequently addressed him,
as Charlton Heston.
   Lots of famous guys
   and gays, wanted to meet him,
   and, of course, treat him.
His feelings for them
were coarsely contiguous,
UNAMBIGUOUS . . .
   But it was ever
   honi soit qui mal y pense,
   in the Renaissance.
His gayness became
greyness, and so the old stick
grew geriatric.
   Death brought its blessings,
   a providence to avoid
   bloody Polaroid.
He, managing to
snuff it, before Yanks and Japs
made him pose for snaps
by the Uffizi . . .
   MIKE WITH JAKE FROM CEDAR FALLS . . .
   and that sort of balls!

RUSSELL LUCAS

LAMBERT SIMNEL (c. 1475–1525)
and PERKIN WARBECK (1474–99)

The Impostors

It was in the fifteenth century,
    A very nasty spell,
When the heads of reigning monarchs
    Like the heads of roses fell,
And everyone was asking:
    'What ruler shall we see?'
And blithely Thomas, Richard, Harold,
With rotten syntax, stood and carolled:
    'It isn't him! It's me!'

Then up spoke Lambert Simnel:
    Of humble birth was he –
'I'm Edward, Earl of Warwick,
    And I will cross the sea
    And your new monarch be.'
'Ha! ha!' cried Henry Seven;
    'Who wants to join the martyrs?
You are a crim'nel, Lambert Simnel;
    I'll have your guts for garters!'

But they crowned him king in Dublin,
    Where anything will go,
And Irish peers with frantic cheers
    Sailed off to meet the foe.
Alas! they went to Stoke-on-Trent
    With Henry to embroil,
But found not only potters make
Objects that very quickly break
    Out of the Stafford soil.
'Simnel,' cried Henry Tudor,
    'You're lookin' so bewitchin'
I'm goin' to save you from the rope;
A turnspit you will make, I hope,
    Within my royal kitchen.'

What followed next may move you
    To laughter or to tears,
For Henry gave a dinner
    Just for the Irish peers,

Where Lambert Simnel, agitator,
Served up the menu as a waiter,
    Truly a masterstroke;
He was a silent commentator
That each had acted like a traitor.
    They did not see the joke.

Now up spoke Perkin Warbeck:
    'This is *my* royal hour;
I am the younger of those
    Two Princes in the Tower.'
King James the Fourth of Scotland
    Helped him to take his chance;
So did (of course) the Irish,
    And Charles VIII of France.

Alas for Perkin Warbeck;
    He was not sent from Heaven;
At first he went to land in Kent
    And then invaded Devon.
'I am King Richard Number Four;
    Come flocking all to me!'
He shouted. But the people swore:
'Your name is Warbeck; furthermore
    You come from Burgundy.'

I have to tell you truly
    Perkin was pretty wet;
He ran away to Beaulieu
    And might have been there yet
Had Henry Seven not promised,
    If he would yield his power,
He would not execute him,
    But keep him in the Tower,
For that was where he'd rested
    Under King Richard Three,
So to it, he suggested,
    He would accustomed be.

A ruthless man was Henry;
    I think he would have found
A good excuse to execute
    Perkin, a king uncrowned;
Or had this feeble uncrowned king
    Some courage to exhibit?

45

For he was caught abandoning
The comfort of his harbouring
And very quickly made to swing
    Upon the common gibbet.

The moral of each story
    Is very much the same:
If you are called John Citizen
    Be happy with your name,
For if you put on airs, my dears,
    And pose as what you're not,
The thing is bound to end in tears;
You'll find that no one cares or hears,
Except, of course, the Irish peers;
    And they're a funny lot.

PAUL GRIFFIN

LUCREZIA BORGIA (1480–1519)

They called me everything beastly under the sun –
You name it; but when all is said and done,
What could a girl expect? I was a Borgia,
Exposed to every hack and scandal-forger.
History romances everything:
Did I keep poison in a jewelled ring?
Did I dispose of husband number two?
Was I my brother's lover? I ask you –
Does it seem likely that a learned lady
Should have to stoop to deeds so dire and shady,
When her father was mighty Pope of Rome,
Her brother feared abroad, likewise at home?
Our enemies were many and mine bore
Me ill-will as a woman, called me whore –
A girl must be ill-favoured and most tame
If she is to escape being given that name
By men whose deeds made Machiavelli queasy –
And that, you will agree, was never easy!
That I was beautiful most will agree,
But this from gossip sets no woman free;

46

Married again, I fostered art and learning,
Though, for this, no Brownie points I'm earning
From philistines: but, in Ferrara, I
Was lauded by great poets – do they lie?
Well, think me what you will. I do not care.
Let's drink to it – that is, if you dare!

MARGARET ROGERS

IGNATIUS LOYOLA (1491–1556)

Our Sole Soul-Soldier

Ignatius, who first forth-fathered our sweet Society,
Guipúzcoa gave brat-breath, whence he grew
Now page, now knight-at-arms five full foot-and-two;
At Pamplona was lég-lámed, which propelled to propriety
This ruddy-polled erst-sinner, 'suaging self-anxiety
In mendicant prayer, self-scourged, nor cried boo-hoo-hóo,
Uncombed nor nailcut; he for Christ, being born anew,
Soldier enlists; manual military penning in penitent piety.

Legged it pilgrim-pace to Jerusalem, Holy City
Of Shalompeace, piecemeal and soul-spacious;
Years-long then of study made he, begging abroad, University
Of Paris him M.A. awarded; ordained to serve our Gracious
Lord; Order then (fond) founded. Last, lived in Rome's vicinity
And tásk done, in 1556, tóok's demob., our revered Ignatius.

GERARD BENSON

47

MARY STUART, QUEEN OF SCOTS

(1542–87)

Dear Mistress Marje,

I don't suppose you often get a letter from a Queen. A real Queen, I mean, not one of *those*. But being a Royal isn't all beer and skittles, and I have problems.

I was born in Scotland and married at sixteen to the Dauphin of France, who was only fourteen. Well, you know what the French are. He was a real wimp; fortunately he died soon after. My mother-in-law, Catherine de Medici, is a real cow. My cousin, Queen Elizabeth of England, is not much better. I had another near relation, Mary Tudor, who was called Bloody Mary by everyone who knew her. So you see I come from a problem family. I am in France at the moment. What do you advise me to do next?

Mary R.

Dear Mary,

First – you don't mind me calling you 'Mary', do you? It's in the true spirit of my column, where I like to think we're all girls together. I think you're better off without your Dauphin. These boy/girl marriages often run on to the rocks. Go back to Scotland, where you'll soon find some nice kind Highland boy who'll help you to forget the past. I expect, with your French background, you can teach those raw Scottish laddies a thing or two! Let me know how you get on.

Marje

Dear Mistress Marje,

I took your advice, returned to Scotland and married my cousin, Lord Darnley. He has turned out to be another wimp. Meanwhile I've fallen for my new secretary, Rizzio – a dishy young Italian. I'm thinking about a *ménage-à-trois*. But would it work in Scotland? They're a bit fussy here – so different from France. By the way, I'm R.C., so do not approve of birth control, abortion, etc. But am otherwise completely broad-minded.

Mary R.

P.S. Terrible shock. Rizzio has been murdered. Foul play is suspected. But who could it be?

Dear Mary,

So sorry to hear your news. Murder is not funny. But look on the bright side. I think you're probably better off without Rizzio. You know what those hot-blooded Mediterranean types are. Advertise for another secretary, but be sure to specify British this time. Do keep in touch.

Marje

Dear Mistress Marje,

More trouble. I've fallen for the Earl of Bothwell. He's a very eligible aristo and mad about me. You didn't answer my question about a *ménage-à-trois*. I've gone off my porridge and feel desperate.

Mary R.

P.S. Another terrible shock. Darnley has been murdered. It's too bad.

Dear Mary,

You do seem to have rotten luck with your hubbies. One murder in the family is bad enough. Two looks like carelessness. Still – look on the bright side. I think you're probably better off without Darnley. Marriage between cousins is not always advisable, on eugenic grounds. With your proven track record you should soon find somebody else. Keep calm. And don't lose your head to the first youngster in kilts who happens to come along.

Marje

Dear Mistress Marje,

'Don't lose your head' you say. That's just what I'm afraid of. Cousin Queen Liz (the Virgin Queen – ha! ha!) is suspicious that I'm plotting against her and has had me locked up. She's C. of E. so she hates R.C.s, but the real reason she's jealous is because I'm much better looking than she is. I've been shunted all round the country from one draughty castle to another, and am now at Fotheringay. Would it be possible to drug my jailers with tranquillizers? Your unhappy Queen of Scots sometimes feels just like any puir ordinary wee lassie, with nobody's shoulder to cry on.

Mary R.

(Mistress Marje's reply to this last letter was returned by the Public Executioner's Office, marked 'Gone away'.)

STANLEY J. SHARPLESS

SIR WALTER RALEIGH (1552–1618)

The Life of Raleigh

A Series of 25 Cigarette Cards

<u>Picture 1</u> – The young Raleigh listens in awe to local sailors discussing what they have brought back from far away countries.

<u>Picture 2</u> – Raleigh asking his father what a 'dose of pox' is and receiving a clout.

<u>Picture 3</u> – The eponymous Raleigh parking his bicycle prior to entering Oriel College, Oxford.

<u>Picture 4</u> – Raleigh disembarking the Sealink ferry to fight for the Huguenot cause in France.

<u>Picture 5</u> – Raleigh serving the Queen in Ireland by knocking the daylights out of the locals.

<u>Picture 6</u> – Queen Elizabeth I giving Raleigh the glad eye at court.

<u>Picture 7</u> – Raleigh collecting his cloak from Sketchley's.

<u>Picture 8</u> – The Queen making Raleigh a knight.

<u>Picture 9</u> – Raleigh making the Queen's night.

<u>Picture 10</u> – Raleigh dispatching a fleet of ships to America with orders to bring back a bag of King Edwards and 20 Benson and Hedges.

<u>Picture 11</u> – The Queen and Raleigh dining on sausage, egg and tobacco.

<u>Picture 12</u> – Raleigh relaxing with a pipeful of Virginian potato.

<u>Picture 13</u> – Raleigh digging his allotment in Ireland while the Earl of Essex cultivates Queen Elizabeth I.

<u>Picture 14</u> – Raleigh discussing affairs with Bessy Throckmorton, the Queen's maid-of-honour. Note the position of Raleigh's hands and the Queen's countenance.

<u>Picture 15</u> – Raleigh visiting the Tower of London – for four years.

<u>Picture 16</u> – Bessy Throckmorton being joined to Raleigh.

<u>Picture 17</u> – Raleigh exclaiming 'Who, me?' after being accused of plotting against King James I.

<u>Picture 18</u> – American tourists queuing to catch a glimpse of Raleigh whiling away thirteen years in the Tower of London.

<u>Picture 19</u> – Raleigh signing copies of his *History of the World* for visitors to the Tower.

<u>Picture 20</u> – Raleigh receiving a phone call from the King requesting him to sail for El Dorado in search of gold.

Picture 21 – Raleigh returning to England empty-handed.
Picture 22 – King James I looking a bit miffed.
Picture 23 – Raleigh in Whitehall sharing a joke with a man in a
black mask.
Picture 24 – Raleigh's body.
Picture 25 – Raleigh's head.

V. ERNEST COX

ANNE HATHAWAY (1555–1623)

'Tis often said that marriage is a lottery,
And wise men everywhere agree that's true;
I married thee, Anne Hathaway of Shottery,
Because there was naught else that I could do.
In very sooth, it seems but yesterday
We lay together in the heaving grass,
And thy low murmur came: 'Anne hath a way
Of getting what she wants.' 'Twas so, my lass.

I sought my fortune then in London town,
Although thou didst not look with favour on it,
And there achieved prodigious renown,
And wrote to a Dark Lady the odd sonnet,
But never doubt thy Will's fidelity,
In proof, my second-best bed I will to thee.

STANLEY J. SHARPLESS

GALILEO GALILEI (1564–1642)

Galileo showed great bottle,
Tangling with both Aristotle
And the prelates of his time
Who decreed research a crime.
Searching with his telescope
In the sky, annoyed the Pope:
'If 'tis in the Book, so be it.'
Galileo urged, 'Let's see it.'
And again if something moved
Smart opinion held it proved ★★
That a force must vivify it.
Galileo urged: 'Let's try it.'
When the Papal team got news
Rumouring heliocentric views
That was it: the Inquisition
Wished to study his position. ★★
'Studying his position' seems
To connote 'until he screams'
Galileo glimpsed the terrors
And recanted from his errors. ★★
His great works and eminence
Stand on planned experiments
Humble methods lead to glory –
Let me show you with a story: ★★
Does a lighter object show a
Tendency to fall much slower?
In the neighbourhood, he knew
Leaned a tower well off-true. ★★
Thus it was, amid great stir,
That his lab assistants were
Standing at the mid-day hour
High on Pisa's leaning tower. ★★
Thud! It came, a single sound
As two bodies hit the ground.
All projectiles, it is clear
Take as long to drop to ...... here.

NOEL PETTY

Twinkle, twinkle, little Earth,
How I wonder what you're worth!
Are your bosses astigmatic?
Do you move or are you static?

Twinkle, twinkle, little brain,
Must your brilliance be in vain?
Galileo Galilei
Muttered: *'Miserere mei!'*

Seems that if I strive to winkle
Information from a twinkle,
In this present age I'm far
From evolving to a star.

I-so-chronically caught
On the pendulum of thought,
See Jove's satellites combine
Just to fault His grand design.

Best enact my earlier teaser:
Leap right off the tower of Pisa,
Paired with an unequal weight,
Falling at as fast a rate.

Twinkle, twinkle little planet,
Seems it's now a crime to scan it;
Forced I may be to forswear –
Blinking thing still moves, so there!

MARY HOLTBY

CHRISTOPHER MARLOWE (1564–93)

The Cautionary Tale of Canterbury Kit Who Went Too Far Too Fast Too Often

Christopher Marlowe (known as Kit)
Grew up to find he didn't fit
His Tudor frame. An atheist,
He took his pleasure getting pissed,
Screwing boys and chewing baccy –
His ways were deemed so wild and wacky,
They sent him down from *Corpus Christi.*
The times were tough; so, to exist, he
Enrolled with Burghley's M.I.5-ers
(Then, as now, a bunch of skivers)
And, through an alcoholic haze,
Started scribbling startling plays,
Notorious for their loose design,
But eloquently 'mighty line'.
His *Edward* (chum of Gaveston) *the Second* –
And *Dr Faustus* too – are reckoned
The real McCoy. *The Jew of Malta*
Is also fun – though some lines falter.
His *Tamburlaine*'s a load of ham though –
The ravings of a mega-Rambo.
At twenty-nine, his life was fucked –
Its motor set to Self-Destruct:
Ahead lay raps for conning, cheating,
Buggery and counterfeiting;
And Walsingham's men were on his track
For double treason (thumbscrews, rack . . .)
Then, supping with one Ingram Frisar
(A Spanish agent in disguise?), a
Row erupted re the score –
And Ingram stabbed him to his core.
Moral: Before the menu-grab,
Decide who's picking up the tab.

MARTIN FAGG

WILLIAM SHAKESPEARE (1564–1616)

ACT ONE, SCENE ONE: Stratford

> [*John Shakespeare worketh at a pair of gloves. Enter*
> *William.*]

WILLIAM: Must I at making gloves turn now my hand
          And dwindle here until the passing of my time . . .?

JOHN: Chuck us that bit of leather, will you?

WILLIAM: When treading sprightly on a simple board
          Compresses all the wonders of the world
          Into a . . .

JOHN: William!

WILLIAM: . . . pregnant hour to make men stand
          And stare and, having stood, to understand . . .

JOHN: Oi! Are you with us or what?

WILLIAM: It's no good. I can't work here. I must find some
          peace.
          [*Exit.*]

ACT ONE, SCENE TWO: Outside Stratford

> [*William museth on a pile of straw.*]

WILLIAM: Bright orb above set now my brain on fire
          And bring forth life where only darkness was!
          [*The straw rustleth.*]
          My dull and country-fed slow-turning brain!
          It teems as doth a stream with silver'd fish . . .

ANNE HATHAWAY: [*From the straw*] Will? What are you up
                to?

WILLIAM: And I, poor fool, know not which way they dart.

ANNE: 'Ere, you got bits of straw sticking out of your hose.

WILLIAM: Oh, this is hopeless!
          [*Exit.*]

ACT TWO, SCENE ONE: London

> [*William and Burbage quaff ale.*]

WILLIAM: 'Tis passing strange that mine invention soars
          Away from Stratford's sleepy banks, and here,
          Here in the thrust and surge of London life . . .

BURBAGE: Quite, quite. Have you finished the play?

WILLIAM: Aye! And full roundly will . . .

BURBAGE: What's in it for me?

WILLIAM: A king! A sage and goodly king who . . .

BURBAGE: Shall I die? I must have a good death.

WILLIAM: 'Shall I die?' I say, Dick, I like the sound of that.

BURBAGE: Forget it. Concentrate on the play.

WILLIAM: I wonder. 'Shall I die?' Hmm.
            [*Exit, musing.*]

ACT THREE, SCENE ONE: Another part of Stratford (New Place)
            [*Enter William and a man with a load of bricks.*]

WILLIAM: Now my long course at least is nearly run . . .

MAN: Where d'you want this lot?

WILLIAM: And all my art is bound into . . . What?

MAN: Where d'you want this lot? You're the man with the money.
            It's up to you, you know.

WILLIAM: This place doesn't change, does it?

ACT FOUR, SCENE ONE: Stratford, the theatre
            [*Shakespeare's ghost queueth for a programme.*]

GHOST: These monied dames in checked and gaudy pants
            With wing'd and ornate structures o'er each eye,
            Clutching the bubble culture . . .

BLANCHE: Are you gonna shift your butt, or what?

GHOST: Pardon?

BLANCHE: Whaddaya think, my friend Phyllis can see through you or something?

PHYLLIS: Actually, Blanche . . .

BLANCHE: Quiet, Phyllis. The guy should move!
            [*The ghost bobbeth down and whispereth.*]

GHOST: Here playeth year by year some sev'ral works
            And some are mine and surely some are not . . .

ACTOR: Must I at making gloves turn now my hand . . .

GHOST: See what I mean?
            Excuse me. I'm so sorry. I beg your pardon. Excuse me . . .
            [*The ghost leaveth.*]

N. J. WARBURTON

56

GUY FAWKES (1570–1606)

Though 'Guido' Fawkes was born in Yorks.
    A Prot. (so say my sources),
Inflamed by Rome he left his home
    To join the Spanish forces.

Back in U.K. where James held sway
    ('The wisest fool' – you've heard it?),
Revolt was smouldering away,
    And crafty Papists stirred it.

It seems one Catesby and his mates
    – A gang of fiery fellers –
The House design to undermine
    By powdering the cellars.

On Guy (unpaid) the charge they laid
    And, fuelled by true piety,
He brought in torches to upgrade
    The leaders of society.

The plot was leaked (a kinsman squeaked);
    They caught him in the dark;
So poor old Guy, defused, must lie
    And lose his vital spark.

His day we keep; why don't we creep
    As Guy Fawkes long ago did,
Set squibs to rouse the House from sleep
    And see some myths exploded?

MARY HOLTBY

The Hollow Man

I am the hollow man,
I am the stuffed man
Leaning back on the trolley,
Collecting the lolly
'A penny for the Guy'.
But years ago
I was stuffed full of knowledge,
I was in the army
Stuffed full of knowledge
About gunpowder.

They got me,
Guy Fawkes,
To do it,
Catesby, Wright and Percy
And other Catholics.
I was the catspaw,
I was to light the fuse
That would blow up
The Houses of Parliament,
Their Protestant King,
Their Protestant Government.

Between the lighting of the fuse
And the explosion
Fell the shadow
Of the soldiers.

Between the arrest
And the trial
Fell the shadow
Of the gallows.
Between the rack
And the screw
Fell the names
Catesby, Wright and Percy.

Between the hanging
And the quartering
Came the drawing.

Between the then
And the now
Have fallen the Guy Fawkes Days,
Have fallen the Bonfire Nights,
The rockets,
The Roman Candles,
The squibs and sparklers,
The Whizz! Bang! Pop!

This is the way my Day ends
This is the way my Day ends
This is the way my Day ends
Not with a whimper, but a BANG!

JOYCE JOHNSON

IZAAK WALTON (1593–1683)

The way that the childhood of Walton was spent is
Unknown till the time he became an apprentice;
His brother-in-law was a draper by trade,
Who his skills to young Izaak with profit conveyed.
The business flourished to such an extent
He was able at last to subscribe himself 'Gent'.
He worked for St Dunstan's when Donne was its priest
And wed a relation of Cranmer (deceased)
So he needed no clergy-connections to fish up
When appointed as Steward to Morley, first Bishop
Of Worcester, then Winchester, where our sketch ends –
Save for all his name stands for, his books and his friends.

Master Walton the draper – his friends made him famous:
The godly and learned, the streamlined and squamous.
He hooked them and landed them, served them up sweet,
All gutted and garnished and ready to eat.
Thus Hooker and Herbert (appropriate dishes),
Donne, Wootton and Sanderson, swam with his fishes:
The Umber, the Barbel, the Dudgeon, the Hogfish,
The Mullet, the Minnow, the Trout and the Dogfish,
The Pike and the Tench and the Carp and the Loach,
The Samlet (or Skegger), the Bream and the Roach.

59

He caught them all fresh on a delicate line
With the Dun-Fly, the Stone-Fly, the Palmer, the Vine,
The Marsh-Worm, the Tug-Tail, the Flag-Worm, the Oak-Worm,
The Lob-Worm (or Wachel), the Gilt-Tail, the Dock-Worm.

Knee-deep in these shoals of evocative names,
The fisherman plays philosophical games,
While hunting and hawking inspire panegyrics
And scholarly milkmaids sing pastoral lyrics.
The *Angler* who offers so varied a treat
Quite rightly entitles his treatise *Compleat*
And when netting his humans (as listed above)
He does so with clarity, vigour and love.
If you've never tried Walton, dear reader, dispatch!
And draw from his cover this succulent catch.

MARY HOLTBY

JOHN MILTON (1608–74)

What was Milton like, O Muse?
Will you let us have your views?
Was he great, or was he so-so?
Allegro, or Penseroso?
Haste thee, nymph, and let us see
Some of Milton's history.

First at Cambridge, Edward King
Died and left him sorrowing.
Further sorrow came, I fear,
When he wed a Cavalier;
Though it gave a certain force
To his writings on divorce.
When the Revolution came,
Pamphlets bolstered up his fame.
Of them all the finest far
Was *Areopagitica*.

Going blind, and twice bereaved,
Via the sonnet form he grieved,
Till the Muse of Epic beckoned
In the reign of Charles the Second.

His filial amanuenses
Hardly could believe their senses,
Having copied quite a nice
Poem about Paradise,
When he thought it would be fun
If they did a second one.
All their grumbling spoilt his life
Till he found another wife.

    Cheerfully, despite his gout,
Then he saw his old age out.
Samson's tale was still to write
Before he joined him in the night.

    A vain and narrow man, we know it;
But what a simply marvellous poet!

PAUL GRIFFIN

COLONEL THOMAS BLOOD (c. 1618–80)

Most of us risk a little loss:
We do the pools or back a hoss,
And, at the best, our labours see
Crowned with a prize of fifty pee;
Yet at the risk of fighting duels
One could abstract the Royal Jewels
And live like some enchanted stud.
So reasoned Colonel Thomas Blood.

No Irishman was ever seen
So Irish as that wild spalpeen.
He backed a loser at the start,
Taking the Parliamentary part,
Lost his estate, and promptly flew
To stage a military coup.
The Duke of Ormonde foiled his plot,
And Blood was very nearly shot.

Seven years later, by some fluke,
He stopped a coach, and seized the Duke;
To Tyburn took the wretched bloke,
Hoping to hang him from an oak;

But there again his effort failed
And into hiding off he sailed.
Now do not underrate the man,
For yet remained his master plan.

These days, within the Tower's heart,
We see the Crown Jewels' counterpart;
For every little girl and boy
Would try to steal the real McCoy;
But then the Jewels were no fake;
What Colonel Blood proposed to take
Offered, in 1671,
A Riviera lifetime's fun.

With three colleagues, our jewel collector,
Disguised to seem a country rector,
Ran off with some of the regalia.
Alas! his effort was a failure:
So loudly people hued and cried –
The Keeper jolly nearly died –
That he was caught and put in clink:
The end of him, you well might think.

But in the state of England's realm,
With Charles the Second at the helm,
Poor Buckingham was blamed instead.
In prison Blood was visited
And pardoned by the man who owned
The Royal Crown that he had boned;
And suddenly what he had done
Seemed just a bit of harmless fun.

Rich now, and influential, Blood
Could not stop rolling in the mud;
Though certainly he had some sport
Living in Charles the Second's court.
'Just ask the Colonel,' they would say;
'He'll see you right, if you can pay.'
Nine years the Fates were on his side
Before he pushed his luck, and died.

Our world has many a denizen
Like Colonel Blood, some Irishmen,
Full of big ideas and glitz.
Not many finish in the Ritz.

A fool, I think, is one who treads
Always on other people's heads.
Wormwood Scrubs is full of fools.
Perhaps we'd better do the pools.

PAUL GRIFFIN

SIR ISAAC NEWTON (1642–1727)

Young Isaac was a country lad, a son of Lincolnshire,
But he didn't reckon farming was a thinking man's career.
So he filled his head with learning and within a year or two
He was stunning 'em at Cambridge with the wonderful things he
                                                        knew.

To every branch of science Isaac Newton turned his hand,
Inquiring into all the things folk couldn't understand.
His law of gravitation was discovered, so it's said,
When an apple dropped off a garden tree and thumped him on the
                                                        head.

The invention of the calculus caused bitter words to flow.
A German named von Leibniz claimed: 'The idea's mine, you
                                                        know.'
But really it was Newton's, so let's give the man a cheer,
For you never could call him a poacher – not the lad from
                                                        Lincolnshire.

Newton never cared for money and at times was frankly skint,
But in sixteen-ninety-nine they made him Master of the Mint.
He sorted out the currency – and by some twist of fate,
His face popped up on the one-pound note at a very much later
                                                        date.

PETER VEALE

63

STRADIVARIUS (ANTONIO STRADIVARI) (c. 1644–1737)

Apprenticed first to Nick Amati,
Young Antonio was smart, he
Set up business on his own – a
Workshop in downtown Cremona.
There his sons and he made Strads,
(But were the lads' as good as Dad's?)

He turned out (est.) at least a thou.
Prize instruments, though Lord knows how;
Perhaps his varnish (softly spread,
Deep orange shading into red)
Might hold the long-sought-after key,
But Tony left no recipe.

And still his noble violins
Support the world's most gifted chins,
And stacks of fiddlers still extol a
Strad-made 'cello or viola.
But he never made a double bass:
Perhaps he didn't have the space.

RON RUBIN

ELEANOR GWYNNE (1650–87)

When Charles the Second met Nell Gwynne,
Discreetly, under cover,
He wanted her, but had a Queen
So took Nell as his lover.
A salesgirl in the Theatre Royal,
Nell glowed with youthful beauty,
Just like the oranges she sold –
Round, full of pith and fruity!
The King, who had a roving eye,
Found Nell was easy on it,
If he'd been William Shakespeare, he'd
Have put her in a sonnet.

She certainly enjoyed herself
As mistress of a ruler,
Who courted her with costly gifts
Bought from the royal jeweller.
The King, though straight as rulers go,
Learned, if his eyes should wander,
Nell's favours promptly were withdrawn,
Which made him ten times fonder!
But when at last Death summoned him,
What made the parting harder
For Nell, she knew she couldn't act,
(She hadn't been to R.A.D.A.!)
So shuffling off this mortal coil,
King Charles left an instruction:
'Let not poor Nellie starve,' wrote he;
This saved her from destruction.
The backing from his highborn chums
Won parts for her so shameless
Portraying all those naughty roles;
Left Nell's own life quite blameless!

DILYS WAVISH

WILLIAM III ('William of Orange') (1650–1702)

From 'Paisley's Potted Guide to the Monarchy'

William of Orange, the grandson of that slippery backslider, Charles I, was born in the good Protestant city of The Hague. He was a good Protestant son to his good Protestant mother – as he would have been to his good Protestant father if that worthy Calvinist had not succumbed, after a life-time of fighting Popery, eight days before his son's birth.

He developed from an exceedingly tractable Protestant baby into a polyglot Protestant student at the illustrious Protestant university of Leyden. In 1672, when that idolatrous papistical megalomaniac, Louis XIV, invaded the Protestant Netherlands, the brave Dutch Protestants elected this Prince of Protestants their Stadholder and Captain-General.

In 1677 he married Mary, the devout Protestant daughter of that foul Romish renegade, James II; and, in 1688, on

65

November 5th (that doubly blessed day!) he landed among the good Protestant burghers of Brixham and marched on London to overthrow his infamous incense-sniffing father-in-law and uncle. (Typically, that lily-livered, yellow-bellied spalpeen James fled without even putting up a fight – just like the papistical little runt he was!)

Thereafter, this good Protestant husband ruled jointly with his good Protestant wife, and was a good Protestant king and constitutionalist. In 1690, he fought that fight that was forever won only yesterday in the hearts of all true Protestants – the never-to-be-forgotten Battle of the Boyne. He died prematurely, after his horse stumbled over a mole-hill. Whether the horse was a papist, or the mole was a papist, or whether they were both in it together, is something that sound Protestant research has yet to discover . . .

MARTIN FAGG

GEORGE FREDERIC HANDEL (1685–1759)

Where'er he walked, fool girls opposed his will;
Men left him flat, and crowded off downhill;
Whate'er he wrote was murdered on the stage,
And all things gathered to incur his rage.
His German birth he placed upon one side,
In England wore an English badge with pride;
But still sopranos fought, and basses strove
To lose the priceless treasure of his love.
When out of favour with King George the First,
His Water Music quenched the royal thirst,
Brought him a pension and a time of grace
Before the opposition gathered pace.
Some mental trouble, and a heart attack,
Made him put opera behind his back;
When, lo, near sixty, he recovered fire
And wrote the greatest work of all – *Messiah*!
His fortunes soared, his constitution sank;
He died, with twenty thousand in the bank.

PAUL GRIFFIN

66

JOHANN SEBASTIAN BACH (1685–1750)

Prelude

In the town of Eisenach
Dwelt the family of Bach,
All musicians of finesse,
But the greatest was J.S.
At the church he stunned the flock
With his brand of hard-baroque;
When the protests got too strong,
Bach upped sticks and moved along.
Armstadt, Mulhausen and Cöthen –
All his jobs went for a böthen
Till he was appointed ruler
Of the Leipzig *Thomas-schule*.
Mighty works of subtle skill
Now poured from his teeming quill:
Every day a new toccata,
Every week a new cantata,
Every Easter-tide a passion,
Suites for every national fashion.
Masterpieces *à la carte*
(No one thought of it as Art),
While his first wife and his second
Found home life was just as fecund,
Flooding the musician markets
With a score of little Bach-ettes.
Keyboard works beyond compare
Show his contrapuntal flair.
Lest this term cause obfuscation
Let me give a demonstration:

Fugue

Sebastian Bach, who wrote The Art of Fugue
    Sebastian Bach, who wrote The Art
        Sebastian Bach, who wrote

Was blessed by Nature with a brain so huge
Of Fugue, would often from a staggered start
The Art of Fugue, could so devise each note

𝄞 That while his thirteen kids swarmed round his knees
3 Provide three players with a different line
𝄢 That though each line pursued a different strain

𝄞 He'd write a fugal passage with such ease
3 So that three melodies would inter-twine
𝄢 Such was the working of his mighty brain

𝄞 That all three players, from a staggered start,
3 And yet, each steering by a separate chart,
𝄢 They still – this was the measure of his art –

𝄞 Arrived together at the final part.
3 Arrived together at the final part.
𝄢 Arrived together at the final part.

NOEL PETTY

JOHN WESLEY (1703–91)

(*Tune:* 'Jerusalem the Golden')

John Wesley's tongue was golden;
    He preached for fifty years
Some forty thousand sermons
    And moved the poor to tears.
A preacher! What a preacher!
    How he could speak the Word;
A more convincing creature
    No man has ever heard.

Before West Ham played football
    Or Spurs received their name,
Great crowds would wait for Wesley
    And celebrate his fame.
Across the length of Britain
    In thousands they would roar,
For once a man was bitten
    He'd travel miles for more.

What hours of exaltation
    Were spent beneath his thrall!

O Methodist precursor,
How strong you made them all!
I wish I were a sticker
  Like people in the past;
Ten minutes of our Vicar
  Is more than I can last.

But when I go to Anfield
  Or sit in White Hart Lane,
I think of old John Wesley
And understand again
The blessings of religion,
  The faith that lights men up,
Though now they fix their vision
  Upon the F.A. Cup.

PAUL GRIFFIN

DICK TURPIN (1706–39)

Dick Turpin was a gentleman,
  A gentleman of the road;
When heavy goods weighed down the wheels,
  He'd help to lift the load.
He lurked in lonely laybys
  And leant from wayside gates,
Extolling vital interests
  Above financial straits.

Dick Turpin was a highway man,
  He'd cracked the highway code;
He signalled those who drove too fast
  And hailed them when they slowed.
On offside lanes he'd track them down –
  No effort was too much –
And demonstrate to all concerned
  How Dick controlled a clutch.

Alas for poor Dick Turpin
  And his sleek black limousine!
An accidental puncture sent
  Him North for change of scene;

From unfamiliar carriageways
    He took a fatal bend,
And horse-power didn't save him when
    He came to journey's end.

MARY HOLTBY

BENJAMIN FRANKLIN (1706–90)

The name of this song is called 'The Clever Clever Man', but that's only what it's called. The name is 'It's My Own Invention', but the song is . . . Benjamin Franklin

I saw a very clever man
    Who looked both good and kind;
He seemed intent upon a plan
    That occupied his mind.
To find out what this good man's aim
    And stop my mind from ranklin',
I boldly went and asked his name;
    He said that it was Franklin.

He talked and seemed to be so full
    Of interesting knowledge,
I asked him where he went to school
    And where and what his College.
'My living, sir, I had to earn,
    For we were short of pelf,
And anything I had to learn
    I found out for myself.'

I wondered who his father was
    And put out one more feeler.
'A humble man,' he said, 'because
    He was a tallow dealer,
Who 'prenticed me when I was not
    Much more than twelve years old
Unto a trade – I learnt a lot –
    And did as I was told.'

'And then you branched out on your own?'
    I asked. (I had intentions
Of getting him all on his lone
    To tell me his inventions.)

But he was thinking of an odd
    Experiment with lightning,
By using some new kind of rod,
    Thus making storms less fright'ning.

'Lightning,' he said. 'Now that is caused
    By electricity.
I had a kite.' – And there he paused –
    'Which taught a lot to me.'
His mind was just a treasure trove,
    He had such comprehension.
'You know,' he asked, 'the Franklin Stove?
    That, too, was my invention.

I aim to benefit mankind,
    All ages and all classes.
I'm very pleased that I designed
    The first bifocal glasses.'
I thanked him for the things he'd done
    For travellers and locals,
But mostly for the latter one,
    For I, too, wore bifocals.

And now, whenever I require
    To light an oil lamp,
Or put more coal upon the fire,
    Because the nights are damp,
I sigh, for that brings back to me
This clever man who came to be
The founder of a Library,
Where for a small subscription fee,
The poor could read as much as he,
Whose very own Academy
Became a University,
Who gained far more than one Degree,
Who found he could make melody
With doh, ray, me, fah, soh, lah, te,
    From glasses and some water,
Whose full Autobiography
Reveals his ingenuity –
    Thank goodness, this one's shorter.

JOYCE JOHNSON

DR SAMUEL JOHNSON (1709–84)

To Mr Eric O. Parrott.

Dear Sir,

    I am much obliged for your unexpected communication, and the two florins contained therein. Being not entirely incognizant of your nice reputation, I am honoured by your solicitation for a brief recollection of my life for your collection of biographies, but somewhat discomposed by a report from our mutual acquaintance, Mr James Boswell, that you would not have approached me, save for his intercession, fearful of what you advertised to many persons, as my uneven temperament and turbulent disposition.

    Sir, I am not a brute beast or a barbarous Turk, but a humble lexicographer who procures a modest and precarious livelihood as a man, nay servitor of letters. Even so, Sir, I am profoundly uncertain whether two florins is sufficient recompense for a dancing bear, let alone a scholar, however moderate his appetite for meat or need for shelter. Had it not been for the advocacy of Mr Boswell, who is my particular friend, I would hardly have set myself to labour for such a wretched sum. Allow me then, Sir, the opportunity to quit your debt in two sentences, a florin a toss as they say. The first: 'I was born in Lichfield in 1709, the son of Michael Johnson, a bookseller, and educated at Lichfield Grammar and Stourbridge Schools, spending some time at Pembroke College, Oxford, but departing without a degree, due in part to the damaged fortunes of my family.' And the second: 'Despite this adversity, I established my reputation as a translator, dramatist, biographer, poet, essayist, editor and lexicographer, receiving a belated M.A. from Oxford in the year I published my *Dictionary of the English Language*, obtaining later an LL.D. from Trinity, Dublin, and in my sixty-sixth year, the degree of D.C.L. from Oxford.' There, Sir, you have had your two florins worth. I will drink a florin to your health and a florin to your presumption. And you shall have no more from Sam Johnson.

    Having considered your other request, I suspect that you have been extravagantly misled by mischievous minds that are determined to abuse my name. As I have ever promoted the cause of religion and morality by my powers of argument and language, I am reluctant to abase my Christianity with any demonstration of manifest vulgarity, however literate or well intended. I must therefore decline to contribute to what by your own puffery is a subversive frivolity, put upon the publick by your publisher, Mr Penguin.

I trust, Sir, that I have not seriously contributed to your discontent. If I have, the remedy is in your own purse and in your venture's propriety.

May I remain, Sir, your most obliged and humble servant,

Sam Johnson

RUSSELL LUCAS

JEAN-JACQUES ROUSSEAU (1712–78)

(*Note to all schools:* In accordance with the general principle of the G.C.S.E. that it shall be more nearly relevant to the needs and abilities of pupils than the exams it replaces, all French Orals will in future be conducted in *Franglais*. *Model Specimen* enclosed.)

Q: Qu'est-ce que vous savez about cet Frog Rousseau?
A: Il était né à Genève et il kicked le bucket près de Paris.
Q: C'est sur le ball. Son caractère?
A: Il était un morceau d'un prick et sa vie était un big cock-up – en plusieurs voies qu'un!
Q: Vous pouvez dire cela encore, mon enfant! Mais, ses livres?
A: Ah oui! Il écrit constamment – hélas!
Q: Au sujet de?
A: Les politiques, les économiques, les morals – et tous cet crap. Mais, le sujet qui l'intéressait le most était toujours le fucking.
Q: Il n'était pas le seul un! Un ou deux titres de ses livres?
A: *Emile* (un droit petit git!) au sujet d'éducation; *Confessions* – au sujet de sex mostly – il était into le SM dans un big way; et *Du Contrat Social* au sujet de liberté, égalité and fraternité et tous cet jazz – il influençait La French Revolution énormément.
Q: Son reputation – dans un mot?
A: Il écrit un peu de good stuff mais beaucoup de bullshit.
Q: Bravo! Vous avez passé avec les couleurs volantes!

MARTIN FAGG

LAURENCE STERNE (1713–68)

Dear Eric O.,

How flattering that you ask me to do the biography of
Laurence Sterne for your forthcoming volume. As you know, he's
quite a favourite of mine. I love his discursive, self-referential,
tongue-in-cheek style (so different from my own rather economical
– Mrs Katie James, my English teacher said, Terse – style). And
he's so funny! As you probably also know – perhaps that's why you
thought of me in particular – I played the part of Sterne in a Radio
3 Drama, diddle-diddle-diddle, smirk, smirk, END OF SELF-
PLUG! However, mustn't ramble on. Laurence Sterne was born
in 1713 (I checked this in the *Ox. Dict. of Quotations*, invaluable
book! – Where else would you find Karl Marx rubbing shoulders
with Bloody Mary?) and was a parson (I got that from the intro.
to my dog-eared *Life and Opinions of Tristram Shandy* – what a
nerve, that title! he discusses everything else *but* – we'll never get
there at this rate, *revenons à nos oignons*) who had a living in
Yorkshire. Incidentally, having blithely taken this on, I found I
knew precious little about the life. A trip to Dillon's put that right;
they really are excellent – wonderful people they employ, I mean,
a most personable young lady *** ****** *** ***** and really
knew the stock, *so* helpful, *so* unlike ****** in Charing Cross
Road, no names no pack-drill, where they think Sterne is a fladge
magazine. (*Nuffus dixit*). He married Elizabeth Lumley and they
had a daughter, Lydia. By the way, I had to lash out £19.95; can
I claim? I've got the receipt. Do you want me to go into the
supposed *affaire* with Eliza Draper? *De mortuis nil nisi bonum* might
apply here. On the other hand, the word limit you gave me is
ridiculous. He had quite an eventful life, what with his travels in
France and Italy, his quarrels with the Bishop of Gloucester and
whatnot. How do you pack fifty-five years into a page? I'm sorry
if this arrives after the deadline. My dear wife, Catherine, sent me
off to buy a new battery for the kitchen clock in mid-flow and I
missed the post. Was ever a man interrupted for such a silly
reason? How is Tricia, by the way? How this (these) trivia would
have amused L.S.! Alas poor . . .

GERARD BENSON

LANCELOT (CAPABILITY) BROWN
(1715–83)

Owning land in days of yore,
Round about 1764,
Needed no terrible mental agility;
You simply sent for Capability
Landscape-gardener Brown.
If your house was falling down,
Or your wife's relations were rather coarse
Or you'd put your cash on the wrong sort of horse,
Or your family tree was small,
Lancelot Brown could fix it all.
Many an eighteenth-century squire
Would pluck his chestnuts out of the fire
At the cost of a line of shoots,
A couple of lakes, and a draft on Coutts,
All arranged with great civility
By Lancelot Brown, called Capability.

If your wife was found with a guest Brazilian
Flat on her back in the West Pavilion,
Or your beautiful niece had gone to Versailles
Without so much as saying goodbyee,
And your son was writing to France a lot,
You speedily sent for Lancelot
Capability Brown,
And everything upside down
Would be perfectly *comme-il-faut*;
Your relations would all be nice to know,
Because they'd see how in-the-swim
You really were to be calling *him*.

Lancelot Brown, O Lancelot Brown,
I'm sure he never let anyone down,
Arranging what he thought with pride
Were natural views of the countryside.

Fashion, when it obtains no more,
Can be a bit of a bore;
Obelisks, grottoes, ruined towers,
Charm for a little, then lose their powers;
But nature, unlike your temple and turret,
Expellas furca, usque recurret –

Which means, however you fork it over,
You never get rid of a field of clover.
So Lancelot Brown still lifts his head
Long after the craze for him is dead;
Yet still I think that craze was more
Than the theory of beauty he campaigned for.
The fact of dealing with Capability
Removed any feeling of sheer futility.

How I wish our own nobility
Could avail themselves of the same facility.

PAUL GRIFFIN

JOSEF HAYDN (1732–1809)

Esterhazy, such a Prince
As never was before or since,
Knew a genius from a shyster,
And chose as his Vice-kapellmeister
The greatest genius he could see,
Father of the symphony,
Joseph Haydn, Mozart's friend,
Source of music without end.
Thus each made his reputation
Till death broke the combination.

When this patron Prince was gone,
Johann Peter Salomon,
Finding Haydn on the loose
In London, put his gifts to use,
Stimulating him to score
Twelve grand symphonies, and more.

Tactfully I tell you now
About relations with his Frau.
She was not a helpful wife;
Yet in music and in life
He was naturally prolific.
Since his marriage was horrific,
As relief from Mrs Haydn
He grew very keen to widen
His acquaintance with sopranos,

And to play on their pianos.
This, while not among the reasons
Why he chose to write *The Seasons*,
Brought about a situation
Suitable for *The Creation*.
He was known, I do declare,
As 'Papa' Haydn everywhere.

PAUL GRIFFIN

ROBERT ADAM (1728–92)

Robert Adam found great fame
In the architecture game.
Having made his pile
In Palladian style
He saved up more,
Did the Grand Tour,
Sketched a bit
In Split
And returned.
His brain now burned
With arts of Greece and Rome.
It went so big back home,
All other-type interiors
Were voted its inferiors.
His neo-classical motifs
And Etruscan-bas reliefs
We label *Adam*. And today
Compliment to him we pay:
Adam fireplaces now glow
In every gas-fired bungalow.

NOEL PETTY

RICHARD ARKWRIGHT (1732–92)

There's a place you'll have heard of, called Preston,
That's noted for North End and Pride;
Where the natives roll eggs – and dine best on –
And where Richard the Thirteenth first cried! . . .
With a swivelling chair and white basin,
Young Richard soon opened a shop,
And cut hair . . . and talked non-stop of racin'
– And then thought it was high time to stop! . . .
As a wig-maker, he next egresses,
And invents some new hair-dyes, that last;
And at fair-grounds he buys ladies' tresses,
To make wigs – which were worn in days past . . .
Then one day, for a change, after dinner,
Dicky Arkwright thought he would invent
A machine that would help the poor spinner,
Which he did – and became a rich gent!
Now the spinners in Chorley said: 'Blow 'im!'
For his spinning-frame caused loss of jobs;
So they burned down his mill, just to show 'im
What the workers can do to the nobs! . . .
Soon, old K.C.s, in Chambers, ad-libbing,
Thought his Patents were not writ in stone;
While the young 'uns alleged he'd been cribbing –
And the Spinning-frame wasn't his own! . . .
But Arkwright said: 'Nay – I'm not frettin' –
I'll build mills till I've made tons of brass,
And learn Grammar – I can, and no sweatin' –
Just to prove that I'm not working-class!'
So the Manor of Cromford he purchased –
With lace curtains, and door-knobs, as well –
And as Sheriff of Derby soon surfaced,
Meeting gentry – and folks who could spell! . . .
Now when George the Third heard about Arkwright,
Doing hand-stands, one day, in his gym,
He said: 'Nay – but yon lad's made his mark – Right,
It's high time I did summat for him!'
So Dick Arkwright was summoned, and knighted,

And grew fat, it was said, like a pig . . .
But His Majesty was most delighted
With his excellent work . . . on the wig!

PASCOE POLGLAZE

NAT BENTLEY ('Dirty Dick') (1735–1809)

In Leadenhall Street at number forty-six,
A warehouse flourished, known as Dirty Dick's,
Kept by Nat Bentley, once the glass of fashion,
Who gave up washing out of thwarted passion.
Though dirty, Dick was quite genteel as well,
And in three languages, but oh! the smell!
Forty years on, he wished to move his berth
And took his stock – spoiled goods, ten thousands' worth –
The mildewed mirrors from the warping walls,
Plague-smitten periwigs and billiard balls,
Bespattered bolts of baize, dust-patterned plates,
Chipped china chambers crashing round in crates.
A woman robbed him in his Shoreditch dwelling.
He travelled off to Scotland, poor and smelling,
To die at the Crown Inn, a broken man –
Not stinking rich, but thoroughly down the pan.

FIONA PITT-KETHLEY

MARQUIS DE SADE (1740–1814)

De Sade! thou should'st be living at this hour:
England hath need of thee to warn young men
That if for perverse sex they have a yen,
They'd better realize thy cruel power
Landed thee in jail; thou escaped death
'Tis true, but wast recaptured, brought to heel,
Imprisoned in the infamous Bastille.
And, at Charenton, mad, breathed thy last breath.
In jail, thy scandalous romances written
Of joys recaptured in tranquillity,
If writ today, might show our porn to be,

Unlike thy *Justine*, quite devoid of style;
And those who by thy sadism are smitten
Find thy books raise standards up awhile.

JOHANN HEINRICH PESTALOZZI
(1746–1827)

Let's be fair – he couldn't *help* being a Switzer –
That race who seem so insufferably smug about living in one of
　　the bitzer
The World no one ever thinks it worth collaring –
But what needs hollering
About is the sheer tedium of the man's writing,
Blighting
The days of all those swotting for some fatuous Dip. Ed. diploma.
'Megabore' would be no misnomer
For *The Evening Hours of a Hermit* – and if that doesn't give you
　　an acute attack
Of brain-death, have a crack
At *Leonard and Gertrude* –
He's a wimp and she's a prude.
Admittedly, in opening the door
Of his own home as an industrial school for the poor,
And in stressing the need to stimulate children's curiosity,
He deserves his innovative niche – but oh, the verbosity!
In fact, like all educational preachers, Pestalozzi
Seems hotsy-totsy
Enough in the study – but gives little to attune
With the experience of trying to hold 35 sixteen-year-olds in a
　　beat-up prefab last lesson on a hot, sticky, Friday afternoon in
　　June.

80

JEREMY BENTHAM (1748–1832)

A memo from Jeremy Bentham:

I was making a few autobiographical notes for your book when
this thought struck me: there must be many, many people whose
lives might be set out in it, and even more who are prepared to
read those lives. This occasioned a second thought: what has my
life to recommend it above these others? This, in turn, led me to
conclude that the highest good lies in the greatest good of the
greatest number. Bearing this in mind, I think you'd better leave
me out, don't you?

N. J. WARBURTON

DR THOMAS BOWDLER (1754–1825)

What dire offence from amorous causes springs
Bold Bowdler knew, and clipped young Cupid's wings;
A task as meritorious as hard;
He pruned to purify our national bard,
And sought with a reformer's zeal to crush
Every expression that might raise a blush.
No more need Juliet fan her heated cheek:
She's left with only half her lines to speak,
Sparing the tender conscience of the nation
All hint of conjugal anticipation.
While Tearsheet tears right off into the dimness,
Fat Falstaff shrinks to unsalacious slimness;
Lear's lurid fancies crave 'an ounce of civet'
And busy Bowdler's on the spot to give it.
(Who calls upon a 'good apothecary'
Of Edinburgh doctors should be wary.)
Hysterica that king described his *passio* –
But what of Desdemona's yen for Cassio
As pictured to Othello by Iago?
The only answer was complete embargo.
'Obliterate profaneness and obscenity,
And genius shines with shadowless serenity':
Such was his creed and such his sacred call;
He even did it to *Decline and Fall*.

We may regret he never chopped up Chaucer,
Whose stories, after all, are rather coarser.
(Others assumed his mantle where the text
Suggests that Chanticleer was over-sexed.)
So bow to Bowdler, dainty miss and madam –
Like Macintosh and Sandwich and Macadam –
To all posterity he leaves his name –
(Theirs but material, this a moral fame) –
A shining sentry at the gates of shame.

MARY HOLTBY

ROBERT BURNS (1759–96)

Young Rabbie Burns was born in Ayr,
A place salubrious an' fair,
In aspect mich like anywhere,
    Tho' somewhat wetter;
But famed because the crumpet there
    Nae toon can better.

In youth he was the very de'il,
He drank an' swore an' danced the reel,
An' oft left panting at his heel,
    Some hapless ghillie,
An' monie a maid kenn'd a' too weel
    His holy willie.

But soon the lad was sair inclin'd
Tae follow the poetic grind,
An' tae his grief he used tae find
    That, every time,
When lofty phrases he'd refin'd
    They wouldna rhyme.

Now when the gentlefolk took tea,
Great talk of Monsieur Rousseau's plea
Tae set the noble savage free
    Was a' the rage.
An' Rabbie fancied he would be
    A rustic sage.

An' so he had this clever ruse:
When strapt for English words tae use
He'd counterfeit a Gallic muse
     An' make some up,
Like mixtie-maxtie, trabbie-trews
     Or thriddlin'-cup.

An' in his verse he had the nous
Tae mention ingle-neuks an' ploughs,
An' write a poem aboot a mouse
     An' a' things puir,
An' even one aboot a louse
     Tae make quite sure.

He leapt o'ernight tae instant fame;
All Edinburgh praised his name
An' monie a stately high-bred dame
     Wad eye him keen.
But trustily he ganged back hame
     Tae wed his Jean.

He failed at farming once again,
An' took a post in Excise then,
But a' the time his fluent pen,
     Fired acid darts
At baillies, preachers, aldermen
     An' a' sich farts.

An' how he wad appreciate,
The wondrous whirligig o' fate,
That raised up sich a reprobate
     To be, I ken,
The freedom-lover's laureate;
     Amen, amen.

NOEL PETTY

NAPOLEON I (Napoleon Bonaparte)

(1769–1821)

Napoleon was a soldier brave,
Who thought that he alone could save
The honour of fair Marianne –
Though he was born a Corsican.
For many years he held in thrall
Most of Europe – though not all –
And while he did he organized
The French themselves with laws still prized.
Now the erstwhile democrat
Had turned into an autocrat,
Crowned Emperor with pomp and pride,
With Empress Josie at his side,
A lady who, I've heard it said,
Knew her onions in bed,
(Though Josephine he would divorce
To marry Austria, in due course)
And relatives moved to high places –
It often happens in such cases.
But soon his luck began to change:
Nelson put England out of range,
And Russia made him rue the day
(He thought the Bear an easy prey).
Even the greatest general must,
Confined to Elba, bite the dust;
But still he can't admit that he
Suffers from mortality,
And like some fitter, younger man
Escapes to woo his Marianne.
'Twas not to be, for now at last
At Waterloo his day is past.
To St Helena he is banished,
And wonders where his glory's vanished:
For though Napoleon was no phoney,
No one could value him like Boney!

MARGARET ROGERS

LUDWIG VAN BEETHOVEN (1770–1827)

1770 on the Rhein,
Bonn first heard my infant whine;
'Music in the genes!' they jested,
As I bawled an F sharp line.
Organ, harpsichord and fiddle,
These I mastered as a lad,
Locked away and forced to practise,
By my lazy Burgher dad.
Twelve years old, I sold some music;
Later, earned my daily crust
Playing on the chapel organ,
Hapless anthems bleak as dust.
Extempore was my real forte,
Gave my hands the keyboard's run,
Played to Wolfgang in Vienna;
He said: 'Ludwig, fab, my son!'
Mother snuffed it, I was chuffed, it
Led to cash from Count Waldstein;
Then he gave a grand piano –
'Write me symphonies,' he said, 'say, nine.'
Took to walking in the country,
Harmonizing in my head;
Writing weirdo music helped me
Lure the *Fraüleins* to my bed.
Love affairs I had in plenty;
Getting spliced was not my bag.
Restlessly profound and brooding,
Not for me some half-wit hag.
Next I met the ageing Haydn,
Never really hit it off,
Spent my days in pranks and quarrels,
Came to praise and stayed to scoff.
Lost my hearing – what a choker!
Masterpieces never heard,
Like my Ninth, whose 'Ode to Joy'
Shows you need not be a turd.
Near the end wrote chamber music,
String quartets of joy and doom;
Pisspot brimful on the piano
Symbolized defiant gloom.

Called to God aged fifty-seven,
Choirs of angels at the gate,
Sang my *Missa* in D major,
As I cursed capricious Fate.
Eternal life's a long time passing,
Writing music for the harp,
God suggests I'm twice immortal,
Not a bad life – mustn't carp.

TIM HOPKINS

WILLIAM WORDSWORTH (1770–1850)

I wandered doleful all my days,
    From Cockermouth where I was born;
A poet with a poet's ways,
    A youth by Revolution torn,
        Until, my childish roaming done,
        I married Mary Hutchinson.

An orphan early, I was sent
    To school at Hawkshead and from there
To Cambridge, though I'd little bent
    For serious study. Freed from care,
        In France I met Annette, drank wine,
        And got a child, Ann Caroline.

Returning at the threat of War,
    Annette and daughter left behind,
I sought, far from the city's roar,
    A place to live in peace of mind,
        And found a cosy country cot
        At Alfoxden with sister Dot.

We sojourned there in peace and joy,
    I swore I never more would roam,
For Coleridge lived at Nether Stowey;
    But then we found a better home,
        Beside the lake at Grasmere, sure
        We'd settle there for evermore.

In fair Dove Cottage, by the lake,
  I wed, at last, my childhood's dear,
And she would sew, and cook, and bake,
  While I wrote verses all the year.
      A happy little group of three,
      Just Mary, Dorothy and me.

Then our four children came along,
  Such an idyllic life we led,
So full of merriment and song,
  Though Dorothy went off her head,
      But I was honoured by the State,
      She made me Poet Laureate.

JOHN STANLEY SWEETMAN

JANE AUSTEN (1775–1817)

I do not know why anyone should be interested in this Miss Austen!' said Lady Catherine. 'She is a person of very little account, the daughter of an impoverished clergyman in Steventon, which is a poor village in Hampshire. I believe there is some claim to gentility on the mother's side. Her brother is a banker, or something of that sort, in London.'

Charlotte wondered a little at this judgement, but made no reply and Lady Catherine continued: 'There was an aunt who committed some kind of felony in Bath, but it was hushed up. Miss Austen is not married although my daughter, Georgiana, tells me that she was almost engaged to be married on more than one occasion. You know I do not approve of young women who remain unmarried.'

Since this was a sentiment with which Charlotte was inclined to agree, she was prepared to venture a comment, but before she could do so her ladyship went on: 'I understand that she set up a home for her mother after her father's death – but that is no excuse. This was in Chawton, a sad, small house at a cross-roads where there can have been little relief from the traffic of the coaches and people passing by but an arm's length from the window. It must have been quite unsatisfactory.'

'Yes, indeed,' said Charlotte, 'but I believe her books have met with some success.'

'Some persons suppose her to be a wit, but she appears to me to be simply a pert young woman,' Lady Catherine sniffed. 'My daughter, Georgiana, has read one of her novels. A trumpery romance called, I believe, *Northington Abbey*.'

'*Northanger Abbey*, Lady Catherine,' said Charlotte.

'That is what I said, Mrs Collins. Some others of her works have quite extraordinary titles sounding rather like works of philosophy than common romances. *Pride and Prejudice*, indeed! What pretension! Furthermore she has allowed them to be published under her own name.' Lady Catherine paused a moment to allow this last enormity to be appreciated, then added: 'And, what is more, Mrs Collins, they are to be found in the circulating libraries.'

JOHN STANLEY SWEETMAN

ELIZABETH FRY (1780–1845)

Though Betsy Fry was busy as a tsetse,
You could never shake her Quaker faith at all;
Originally Miss Gurney, she was like the Lord's attorney,
And believed she had a fundamental call.

Though sickly, she was never known as prickly,
Had a masochistic, mystic sort of glow,
Was a little melancholic but a thorough workaholic,
Who took on the prison system as her foe.

Conviction came when seeing the affliction
Of the women thrown unknown in Newgate gaol –
And the incident which riled her was to see them strip a child, a
Little corpse to clothe another, barely hale.

Her attention to her women caused dissension,
But they couldn't libel Bible-busy zeal;
And they knew she wasn't fooling when she gave the women
    schooling,
So they struck a rather grudging sort of deal.

The lock-up laws she thought a kind of cock-up,
Didn't halt her other, mother's role – she bore
Eleven little kiddies, quite enough to make one giddy,
Had she not thought labour what her life was for.

She travelled, and she regularly cavilled –
At the crazy fate the state bequeathed the mad;
And the European purses she demanded pay for nurses,
Refusing to be fobbed off as a fad.

This Norwich lass, who saw the shocking porridge,
Set a higher standard, handed on today;
Though she thought of class as Godly, and she spelt – well, rather
    oddly,
One is glad she had her firm, determined way.

BILL GREENWELL

GEORGE GORDON NOEL, LORD BYRON (1788–1824)

In Extremis

In Missolonghi, foulest of foul towns,
    I lie, while those I came to fight for squabble
Or fawn or cheat. I give my life for clowns,
    Who'd shame the liberty they seek – a rabble
Of venal cut-throats. Fleering Bathos crowns
    My odyssey . . . what's that my medics gabble?
The healing ministrations of these Greeks
Would wreck the most resilient of physiques!

I mend, they claim. Claptrap! No lies deceive a
    Dying man. I'll ask of fate no favour;
And tho' I wish a bullet, not a fever,
    Had finished me, I'll not repine. I waive a
Hero's death – God knows I'm no believer
    In piecing out a life that's lost its savour;
But, scribbler ever, still, while breath's frail taper
Flickers, I'll scrawl . . . Fletcher,* fetch some paper!

My boyhood first – bedevilled by my mother,
    A sentimental tyrant, who would flay
Unwitting faults with fiendish words; then smother
    Her bruised bewildered boy with kisses. May
Her tortured shade find peace! I'll make no pother
    About young wounds, mere prologue to the play –

In which Mama alternately would be a
Fond Niobe – or else, a fell Medea!

At Aberdeen we lived, then Newstead Abbey,
    (By now I was, *aetatis* ten, a peer)
A Gothick pile magnificent yet shabby,
    For we were poor. A civil grant made clear
My path to Harrow. There, tho' lame, not flabby,
    I lazed and sported – had my fill, I fear,
Of feasting, fighting, flirting, fucking, flogging –
What other schoolboy haps are worth the logging?

To Cambridge next, the spacious courts of Trinity;
    And there, in choirboys' charms, discovered that
Though Woman was my constant high divinity,
    I craved boys' bodies too. How dull and flat
To bed one sex alone – sheer asininity!
    Nihil (between delicious sheets) *obstat* –
A Byron who'd eschewed the sweets of sodomy
Would be a much more doddery, much odder me!

Pursued by debts, I sought a warmer clime,
    And drank deep draughts of lush Levantine pleasure.
I swam the Hellespont; and all the time
    Stored up in sonorous verse my traveller's treasure.
Back home, two Cantos saw the light. For rhyme,
    Fame's ladled out in scant or giant measure:
The crabbiest, most captious critics carolled
High Paeans for my Muse's 'Childe', glum 'Harold'.

A lion then, the spoiled prey of Venus –
    All London my serail! Poor Caro Lamb,
Fond Lady Oxford's 'autumn charms' . . . No penis
    Ever stood to arms so often. A ram
Were chaste beside . . . How faint and far that scene is
    Now! Of brave Augusta's plight I still am
Loath to speak – must be elliptic, lest you fuss
A brother's cryptic ardour grew incestuous.

My marriage is too sore a tale to tell
    Again. Suffice, that her I dreamed my angel,
Transformed into a harpy hot from hell,
    Arraigned me basely. Failed love's a tangle
Of lancinating wrath and pride. We fell
    To rancour, curses, squalid lawyers' wrangle.

'Those years I've left,' I vowed, 'shall all be on
Some other shores than those of ingrate Albion.'

I must be brief, for Death will shortly come
   (I even hear the stolid Fletcher sigh!')
Geneva, Venice, Pisa, Florence, Rome,
   Became in turn my caravanserai.
Ravenna, with Teresa, was my home –
   And then I heard this anguished people's cry . . .
What dolt could view his dissolution bitterly,
Who's lived so long and blissfully in Italy?

How can I, in a stanza's span, compress
   My urgent, errant days? Say this: 'Unmoved
By maxims, ever counting virtue less
   Than sympathy, he often sinned, but proved
A friend, in need, in deed, to man's distress.
   He loved in legions – was by legions loved.
Now, at the hour when he and life must part,
Say *aught*, say *all* – *save* that he lacked a heart!'

MARTIN FAGG

* Fletcher, referred to twice in these stanzas, was Byron's ever-faithful if often-
infuriating servant. From the fact that the verses were discovered, early in 1987, by
a firm of house-clearers, in the Peckham home of one of Fletcher's remote
connections, it would seem that Fletcher himself had abstracted the filthy and well-
nigh indecipherable sheets on which they are scrawled from his master's death-bed.

M.F.

WILLIAM BURKE (1792–1829)
and WILLIAM HARE (dates not known)

A young Irish navvy called Burke
And a lodging-house keeper called Hare
Went down to Greyfriars to lurk,
And dig out the stiffs buried there.
When the tombs were all empty they murdered Hare's lodgers,
Prostitutes, layabouts, drunks and old codgers.
Then they took them to Knox, stripped and sewn up in sacks,
And he gave them much gold as his morals were lax,
Till the courts hanged Will Burke for his part in this work,
(As disclosed by Hare). And thus ended the pair.

FIONA PITT-KETHLEY

THOMAS BABINGTON, LORD MACAULAY (1800–1859)

List all ye tender poets
Who spin your fragile dreams,
And hear a tale of yesteryear,
When poets wrote in reams.
Hark how the silver stanzas
And golden periods rolled,
When great Macaulay turned them out
In the brave days of old.

Young Thomas was precocious,
Contriving to create
A *Universal History*
Before the age of eight.
Twelve books of *Fingal* followed
(A modest teenage thing)
And then at Trinity he won
The prize for Everything.

The bar was rather boring,
The northern circuit dim;
He thought the literary life
More suitable for him.
He knocked a piece together
On Milton's life and work;
It made the *Edinburgh Review*
And critics went berserk.

By now a social lion,
Loquacity his bent,
He promptly did the decent thing,
And entered Parliament.
His maiden speeches launched him
On a glittering career,
And e'en the ranks of Torydom
Could scarce forbear to cheer.

His acolytes regarded
His mighty mind with awe –
Historian, critic, poet, sage,
And Secretary for War.

And from his pen there issued
Tome upon weighty tome,
From India's constitution
To *Lays of Ancient Rome.*

And still the stanzas gathered,
And still the epics grew;
The *History of England* came
Vol I and then Vol II.
'God grant him,' cried Lord Melbourne,
'The strength to drive his nib on,
For such a gallant feat of words
Was never seen since Gibbon.'

Vols III to V soon followed
But weariness began,
And though he got through William,
He couldn't manage Anne.
And when he ceased his labours,
And let Death have his will,
The word went out throughout the land:
The golden tongue was still.

Such mealy-mouthed professors
As genius attracts,
Have sometimes said his rhetoric
Was stronger than his facts.
But still when writers gather,
Let then the tale be told
Of how Macaulay churned it out
In the brave days of old.

NOEL PETTY

CARDINAL JOHN HENRY NEWMAN
(1801–90)

That's my first incarnation on the wall:
Anglican Vicar, or some such; the style
Not quite as colourful as that I own,
Here in the bosom of the timeless Church.
I had it painted when I caught myself

Longing for truth. At Cambridge, Sir, you read
My *Apologia Pro Vita Sua*?
I'll not repeat what there I said, to shame
An adversary unworthy of my pains:
Kingsley his name, a muddled hearty man,
Expert on Water Babes, I do not doubt,
But lost in argument.
                    Now look, my royal Sir,
On me as Cardinal, the shades of red
Marking the sunrise of my later fame.
You say my first was greater? that the Church,
So-called, in which my early years were spent,
Grows strong because of what I said to it?
You like the early picture? Very well;
Augustine's City stands on paradox;
God's mercy may extend to former selves
As well as latter. *Amor vincit omnia.*

I thank you for your visit, Sir, and pray
One day you may hear Mass in sacred Rome,
With the approval of your royal mother.

PAUL GRIFFIN

ELIZABETH BARRETT BROWNING
(1806–61)

How I Brought the Good Liz from Walpole Street to Florence

I wrote to my Lizzie and Liz wrote to me,
We wrote and we wrote and I wanted to see
If she, like her poems, was clever and pure:
I determined to meet her, though she was unsure.
I called at the house, was admitted at length,
And there lay my Liz, sadly lacking in strength.

Mr Barrett, her father, a tyrant no less,
Kept the motherless family in frightful duress:
My Lizzie, his favourite, upon her couch lay,
Not daring to cross him, not moving all day.
But I was determined that Lizzie should be
Mrs Browning, and saved from her father by me.

94

So I got her to walk and I got her to say
She'd elope with me, marry me, flee far away:
This we did and in Florence Liz lost her old fears
And gave birth to a son and, for full fifteen years,
We lived the good life and we wrote poetry;
Then Elizabeth died and left Junior to me.

MARGARET ROGERS

EDGAR ALLAN POE (1809–49)

From Boston, Massachusetts, on
    The distant western shore,
Came a sad and eerie poet,
    Ever dreaming of Lenore –

Or Annabel – or Ullalume –
    And many more of them,
And all were like his youthful bride,
    The lost Virginia Clemm,

Or like his girlish mother who
    Had died when he was three –
So lovely in her coffin, surely
    Dead she could not be?

Poor orphan, then adopted as a
    Wealthy merchant's child,
And then expelled from college as
    Undisciplined and wild.

By women, wine and gambling lured,
    So swift was his descent
That finally his father cut
    Him off without a cent.

Then haunted by a Raven with
    A very one-track mind,
He scared himself, and us, by tales
    Of rather sombre kind,

95

With bells and pits and pendulums,
  And whirlpools in the waves,
And lovely maidens laid to rest
  Still living in their graves,

And wrote and wrote away for years,
  To keep his fading bride,
And went to pieces afterwards –
  Of dope and drink he died.

Yet, what with psychopathic apes
  With superhuman powers,
And necrophilian dentistry
  In churchyards after hours,

The one-eyed cat who took revenge,
  (And Puss, I think, was right),
And Roderick Usher *and* his house
  Collapsing out of fright –

Although the Poet's weaknesses
  And vices some deplore,
The Hammer House of Horror will
  Be thankful evermore.

O. BANFIELD

EDWARD FITZGERALD (1809–83)

Myself now old am still the Suffolk-born,
Have been to London once or twice, but scorn
  To venture where the Sufis weave their Spells
And Minarets the cloudless Skies adorn.

They say the Lion and the Lizard sit
In far Irán; I do not care a Bit.
  I talk to Sailors on the Aldeburgh Beach,
And that's about the Length and Breadth of it.

The Bulbul sings, and suddenly I flinch;
I think: 'I'd go to Persia at a Pinch';
  But no one knows, and I the least of all,
Whether it was a Bulbul, or a Finch.

Jamí is dead; and I have laboured long
To turn his mighty Tale into Song,
    Of Sálamán and Absál; but who knows,
As with the Bulbul, if I got it wrong.

For old Khayyám, my Treatment was the same,
And that has brought me not a little Fame.
    With Persian Scholars I shall not contend;
People grow tired of Claim and Counterclaim.

A joint of Lamb, a Pint of Beer, and Thou,
Khayyám of Naishapur, I will allow
    To pay for them; but for the Rest
Woodbridge to me is Wilderness enow.

The Bulbul sings; perhaps it is a Lark.
The Roofs of Woodbridge redden and grow dark.
    I do not care for Bulbuls; Adnams Ale
And Sailor Boys are really more my mark.

Let old Fitzgerald your Example be,
Who spends his Life in Suffolk by the Sea,
    In Khorasán may Sultán Máhmoúd reign;
I have invited Tennyson to Tea.

PAUL GRIFFIN

CHARLES DARWIN (1809–72)

As a youngster Charles Darwin collected
Lots of birds of the types now protected,
    Spiders, beetles and bugs,
    Daddy-long-legs and slugs . . .
While his normal school work was neglected.

After Cambridge, on H.M.S. *Beagle*,
He examined a bald-headed eagle
    And discovered the reason
    Why, even in season,
It never could mate with a seagull.

97

Then, discarding all circumlocution,
He faced up to the final solution,
    That the shape of Mankind
    Is decreed and defined
By the principles of evolution.

You can hardly believe the sensation
That was caused on the first publication
    Of his 'Origin' – Why?
    Well, it seemed to imply
That the monkey was Man's close relation.

From the pulpits priests thundered objection
To the doctrine of Nature's selection,
    And it's said there were some
    Who were so overcome
They forgot to take up a collection.

All the Press and both Houses were furious
And condemned his assertions as spurious.
    He was snubbed at his club
    And thrown out of a pub –
A circumstance known to the curious.

In the streets every unlettered peasant
Would indulge in some gesture unpleasant,
    With perhaps a short mime
    Of an ape's breeding time –
Provided no ladies were present.

Unabashed by such childish effusions
And amused by such vulgar allusions,
    Darwin said, with a smile:
    'Mankind's critical style
Merely serves to confirm my conclusions.'

T. L. MCCARTHY

FRÉDÉRIC CHOPIN (1810–89)

Frédéric Chopin
Pianist and Pole
Lover, composer,
Consumptive soul,
Taking a romantic
View of his role,

Made with G Sand,
Novelist, talker,
Un ménage à deux
In sunny Majorca.

There he devoted
Long summer days
Writing Mazurkas
In nostalgic haze
And, after supper,
The odd Polonaise.

He could, if sad,
Tormented, lonely,
Write *Études* for
Black keys only.

Then if his heart
Was happily in it
Knock out a waltz
Duration 1 minute
Clear as the dew,
Fresh as a linnet.

Pianists boasting
Prehensile hands
Beat it to death
On concert grands.

NOEL PETTY

ROBERT BROWNING (1812–89)

You'ld know my life? Zooks! Then I'll spill ('s they say)
　　The beans. Having been born in Camberwell,
(You know it? sure, sure) on the sev'nth o' May
　　In eighteen-twelve, I grew and learnt; I'll tell
You all. Wait, wait, my friend, don't go away!

These details are the soul o' th'telling, friend,
　　So hear me out; born in Southampton Street
In eighteen-twelve . . . I told you? Heav'ns forfend!
　　It seems that in my dotage I repeat
Myself. Well, let it pass. I wrote, yea, penn'd

Poems and Plays. It seems that I was read.
　　I met Elizabeth. We loved. *Finite*.
Our passion was but glorious. We wed.
　　(In Marybone), to Pisa then took flight.
We loved. She died. And now I too am dead.

GERARD BENSON

EDWARD LEAR (1812–88)

There once was a person called Lear
Whose status is somewhat unclear,
　　For most think his name
　　Is entitled to fame
Just for this which I illustrate here.

Though of genius this may be a fitter sign,
One ought not all glory to it assign;
　　Zoological art
　　Was his line at the start
And his sitters were frequently psittacine.

His paintings such talent displayed
That a nobleman came to his aid:
　　'Dear Lear, are you willin'
　　To practise your skill in
My home – and in Rome – if I paid?'

This he does; and for children designs
Brief verses whose span he confines
    – Though the space is made bigger
    To fit in a figure –
To five biographical lines.

This 'Nonsense' was followed by songs
About Jumblies and Pobbles and Dongs,
    And that fine pair of beasts
    To whose runcible feasts
An immortal aroma belongs.

Meanwhile throughout Europe he'd ride
And take Egypt and Greece in his stride
    – Few landscapes escape a
    Transmission to paper –
Till at last at San Remo he died.

To the days of his pilgrimage here
This depressive brought beauty and cheer,
    And readers hereafter
    Shall cry through their laughter:
'How pleasant to know Mr Lear!'

MARY HOLTBY

'How unpleasant to know Mr Foss!'
    Said the world: 'He's so terribly scratchy!'
I think he'd a right to be cross
    With Lear for his Saatchi and Saatchi.

Lord Derby's grandchildren for hours
    In rapturous merriment sat
At Edward's nonsensical powers,
    With never a thought for the cat.

They gasped when he wielded his brushes;
    For Lear as a painter was fine –
Of landscapes, and daisies, and thrushes –
    And he never distorted a line.

But he simply would not flatter felines;
    When he drew with his cat on his desk.
His pen made habitual beelines
    For the odd, and remote, and grotesque.

It must have made Foss very crabby
    To see him paint beautiful birds
But not do the same for his tabby,
    When he might have moved all to these words:

'Debonair as a slim Della Robbia,
    And sleeker by far than his boss,
That redoubtable animal lobbier;
    How pleasant to know Mr Foss!'

PAUL GRIFFIN

GRACE DARLING (1815–42)

Grace, the lighthouse-keeper's daughter,
Rescued five in stormy water;
Girls who get a kick from *Lace*
Aren't the type to envy Grace.

MARY HOLTBY

WALT WHITMAN (1819–92)

I, Walt Whitman, poet and ranter, singer of myself in the rhythms of
    my own America,
Will, me myself and I, inscribe my own life, the biography splendid,
    the Odyssey of an independent soul.

I was born in Paumanok, Long Island, in eighteen hundred and
    nineteen, descended from the English and from the Dutch.
One of nine children, I formed soon my bond with humanity,
For I am all men and all women *et cetera et cetera* (see *Leaves of Grass*
    for further details),
For we removed to Brooklyn during my infancy,
For when I was twelve years old I started work, learning the printers'
    explicating trade,
For I taught in schools,
For I edited the *Brooklyn Eagle* but was awarded the sack and went
    thence to New Orleans.

Did I have an *affaire* with a Creole woman?
Was I a homosexual?
Wouldn't you like to know?!

I invented a new method of poetry, very rolling and American
But nobody would print it and make it public,
I sold a house and myself published the first edition of *Leaves of
     Grass*,
And this became very addictive,
For I produced a second edition and then a third,
And later a fourth and a fifth edition,
And to cut a long story short,
Which is something I rarely did,
There were nine editions in all, each one different from the others
And getting bigger and better all the time.

In the American Civil War I cared for the wounded men
And afterwards worked in the Department of the Interior, but was
     again fired,
For being the author of a notorious book.
How can there be notoriety in stating what is open, manly, frank and
     true?
Pretty easily, seemingly.
However, I found fresh employ in the office of the Attorney-
     General.

I, a big healthy man, generous of thew and limb, florid of counte-
     nance,
Was stricken in my fifty-third year with paralysis,
But for many years lived on, with a little help from my friends.

For I am a son of America!
And it took a conglomerate of ailments,
In the lungs, the stomach, the liver, the kidneys, to finally carry me
     off,
Evangel-poet, habitant of Camden, New Jersey,
In the March of eighteen-ninety-two.

And I will tell you this:
To die is different from what anyone supposed, and luckier.

GERARD BENSON

FLORENCE NIGHTINGALE (1820–1910)

Don't let your daughter be a nurse, Mrs Nightingale,
Don't let your Flossy flush the pans.
It's unbecoming her station
To moot such mutinous plans –
She'd better serve the nation
By tittling and tattling
And prettily prattling
Of nuptial bells and banns.

Don't let your girlie tend the troops, Mrs Nightingale,
Don't let your treasure tread their wards.
The work's so *frightfully* squalid – a nice girl shirks and shuns
Repairing the rents of sordid swords
And those nasty, noisy guns!

Regarding yours, dear Mrs Nightingale,
Of Friday, the 4th of May –
W.at can I candidly say –
No *wonder* you're deep in dismay!
Altho'
Dear Flo
Is clear in her tiny mind
That this gruesome grisly grind
Is her Destiny designed –
How shall we tell
The foolish gel
That a nurse is a slut, a Jezebel,
Whose lot is an utter, gutter hell
Of mangling and mopping
And sluicing and slopping
Out patients who – frankly –
Sweatily, dankly –
Only too rankly
SMELL!

But she's off, so you say, to that *dreadful* Crimea!
I'm terribly vague about Russia, I fear,
But wasn't that where Colonel Darcy de Vere
(His privates *adore* him – an absolute *dear*!)
Was taken so shockingly, shamingly queer –
And poor Lady Mabs nearly died of diarrhoea?

Or was it perhaps in Odessa?
No matter the place – what is totally clear
Is that Flo must say NO! – she must *not* persevere,
I cannot think what can *possess* her!

So don't let your daughter be a nurse, Mrs Nightingale,
Don't let the reckless wretch rebel.
She'll sink to a social pariah,
Cast far beyond the pale;
So harden your heart and try a
Pitiless diet of bread and water –
Try soundly *whipping* your dutiless daughter –
And make her Home her Jail.
Be *bossy*, Mrs Nightingale – foil Flossy, Mrs Nightingale,
AND DON'T LET THE HUSSY BE A NURSE!

MARTIN FAGG

WILLIAM McGONAGALL (1825–1902)

It was in the Spring of 1825 *
That poet McGonagall commenced to be alive.
He spent his youth in various Scottish towns,
Where his father laboured for meagre half-crowns.
William had a gift for tragic recitation
Which later became famous throughout the nation,
But it was in bonnie Dundee city
That he composed his first poetic ditty.
This was in Dundee holiday week, June 1877,
When a voice commanding him to write came from Heaven.
Though William as a poet had developed late,
His flood-gates were open wide by July 1878,
When he presented himself at fair Balmoral's gate
To offer his poetry to the Queen sitting in state,
In hope of one day becoming Poet Laureate.
His sharp rebuff on that sad day
Did not cause him undue dismay,
And he continued on his poetic way

* McGonagall himself 1830 as his birth-year states,
  Which is odd for someone so obsessed with dates.

With his famous *Beautiful Railway Bridge of the Silvery Tay*,
Followed by another on that bridge's sad demise
Amid the passengers' woeful cries
On the last Sabbath day of 1879
(Which will be remembered for a very long time).
In March, 1887, he set out in search of further fame
To far New York, but finding that none came,
He returned to Dundee without delay
Just in time for the opening of the New Railway Bridge across the
    Tay.
Verses on all state occasions now poured from his pen,
Together with a strong line in all disasters known to men.
He survived long enough Edward VII's coronation to review,
Which was on August 9th 1902,
But the poet's sad death soon after unfortunately occurred,
To be precise on August 23rd.

NOEL PETTY

WILLIAM BOOTH (1829–1912)
and CHARLES GEORGE GORDON (1833–85)

(*Tune:* 'Austria', F. J. Haydn)

General Gordon was a soldier,
 Sword and Bible in his hands.
Taking British peace and justice,
 Into many heathen lands.
William Booth was not a soldier,
 Not a military man.
Since his father was a preacher,
 As a preacher he began.

Gordon fought in the Crimea,
 Then to far Cathay he came,
Sacked Peking and smashed the rebels,
 'Chinese Gordon' he became.
Booth came down to preach in London,
 Worked for justice, truth and right,
Formed his own Salvation Army,
 Gladly fought the Gospel fight.

Gordon did great work in Egypt,
    Lightening the people's gloom,
'Til the Mahdi's hordes o'erwhelmed him,
    And he died there in Khartoum.
General Booth and General Gordon,
    Knew alcohol must lead to sin.
How sad it is their names remind us
    Of Britain's leading brands of gin.

JOHN STANLEY SWEETMAN

EMILY DICKINSON (1830–86)

She lived – almost Alone,
    A Lady – frail and small.
Her life in Monotone,
    No peaks – no troughs at all.

Was she once Crossed – in Love?
    Did Someone – leave her Flat?
Cast like an out-worn glove,
    All in a Flash – like that?

A quiet New England – Miss,
    For Fame – she did not Care.
She often wrote – like This,
    With Dashes – everywhere –.

She Wrote no – Public Verse,
    Restraint was all her Art.
Her poems rather – Terse,
    Tho' written – from her Heart.

'Tis easy to deride
    Her very Private Tongue.
She Died – as she had Lived,
    Unhonoured – and Unsung.

JOHN STANLEY SWEETMAN

REV. CHARLES LUTWIDGE
DODGSON ('Lewis Carroll') (1832–98)

'You are old, Mr Dodgson,' the young man said,
  'And I do hope you'll not be annoyed
If I point out that much of your work could be read
  As a classic case-study by Freud.'

'In my youth,' said the cleric, 'I channelled myself
  Into mental games, maths and divinity;
When I came up to Oxford, I'd left on the shelf
  The whole problem of my masculinity.'

'So when Alice falls down,' the young man pursued,
  'A dark tunnel . . . I don't wish to vex,
But would you agree that your stories exude
  Pathological fears about sex?'

'In my youth,' said the cleric, 'I knew naught about
  The liaisons of young men of leisure,
And – although I don't *quite* like your tone – there's no doubt
  That I've never – ahem! – had the pleasure.'

'You are old,' said the youth. 'I don't wish to be rude,
  Since your good name is spotlessly white,
But you constantly photograph tots in the nude –
  Do you honestly think this is right?'

'Being modern,' the cleric said crisply, 'you feel
  Such a hobby suggests paedophilia;
But since innocence is the Victorian ideal,
  Your assumption could scarcely be sillier.'

'One last point,' said the young man, 'and then we'll play chess.
  Don't suspect me of harbouring malice,
But is this an unconscious attempt to regress?
  Do you see *yourself* mirrored in Alice?'

'You are right,' said the cleric, with eyes sad and mild,
  'And to this crime I willingly own up;
For, compared with the glory of being a child,
  Where's the virtue in being a grown-up?'

PETER NORMAN

LOUISA MAY ALCOTT (1832–88)

'You'll never guess where I've been!' said Jo breathlessly, as she unbuttoned her cape and, at once, went on: 'I've met our new neighbour, she's called Miss Alcott and she comes from Philadelphia and she wrote her first diary when she was only four, but when she was little she fell in the pond on Boston Common and would have drowned if a black man hadn't pulled her out; and that's why she went to be a nurse in the War, and she's been to Europe, and her father and her had all sorts of grand friends like Mr Emerson and Mr Thoreau, and she's a writer; she's had lots of books published about just ordinary people and she's interested in women's suffer . . ., suff . . .' Jo paused, momentarily lost for a word, and Beth broke into sobs. 'O! poor women, suffering so!' she said and shed a small crystal tear. 'Don't cry, Beth,' said Meg. 'Jo means suffrage, not suffering, that's only about votes at elections.' 'I know that,' said Jo, rather sharply, 'I just lost a word. She's written books and books about American people just like us. She's frightfully clever.'

Just then Mrs March came in. 'I'm so glad you've met Miss Alcott, Jo dear,' she said. 'Her father, Mr Bronson Alcott, had a house at Fruitlands and he was a great reformer, though some of his ideas were rather odd. But, in these days when so much of what is written is rather unsuitable, it is good that a lady can write books that are morally satisfactory and still reach so many people. *Little Women* is, I think, the best of her books; I have a copy upstairs which you may read.' Mrs March paused, and then continued: 'Miss Alcott had three sisters, you know, and one of them was called Elizabeth.' Beth smiled at this and Mrs March forbore to add that Elizabeth Alcott had died when she was quite young.

JOHN STANLEY SWEETMAN

SAMUEL LANGHORNE CLEMENS ('Mark Twain') (1835–1910)

Citizen Twain

I had the remarkable good fortune to be present at my own birth. Arriving in the world in 1835 precisely, I found myself in a small shop in Florida, Missouri. The shopkeeper and his wife introduced themselves to me as my father and mother respectively and informed me I was called Samuel Langhorne Clemens (Sam for short – but not for long). My entire childhood was spent researching material for a couple of best-sellers I intended to write. At twelve I made it into print – as an apprentice compositor with the *Missouri Courier*. When I had tired of being a man of letters, I decided to train and become a pilot. Aeroplanes hadn't been invented yet, so I settled for a Mississippi steam boat. I quit the river to join in the Civil War as a Marion Ranger, but was too late to be allocated a horse and deserted from exhaustion when I couldn't keep up with the rest of the cavalry. Next I tried gold mining, but it offered no prospects and I fell to writing. I figured it might be tricky fitting Samuel Langhorne Clemens on book covers, so I adopted an orphaned pseudonym and made my mark under the name of Twain.

If you have ever bought a copy of my *Tom Sawyer* or *Huckleberry Finn* I offer you my sincere thanks. The money I made from those two books helped pay off debts I incurred when my publishing company crashed.

Figuring that moving targets are the hardest to hit, I spent a good part of my life travelling around and changed jobs as often as some women change their minds.

On the basis of 'if the cap fits . . .' I accepted an honorary doctorate in Literature from Oxford, England. Well, people have called me the Yankee Charles Dickens. Personally, I prefer to think of Chas. as the Limey Mark Twain.

I died in 1910, just a few days before my own funeral, so was unable to be there in person. Still, better late than never.

V. ERNEST COX

SIR WILLIAM SCHWENK (W.S.) GILBERT (1836–1911)

He was the very doyen of linguistical dexterity,
Gave music muscularity, lampoonery legerity;
Before he found his natural bent and made a lite*rary* stir
Entirely unsuccessfully he practised as a barrister;
His fees fell short of keeping him in steakery and saladry,
So he earned some extra pennies by the exercise of balladry:

His *Bab* – a work of genius both verbal and pictorial –
Might stand without addition as a suitable memorial,
But if the Ship of Song required an expert bottom-copperer
She found him in our hero when he turned to comic opera.

Bab Ballads had a sequel, for their author didn't dully van-
ish into mere obscurity, but joined a chap called Sullivan;
With D'Oyly Carte as backer, of their craft collaboratory
The early *Trial by Jury* was a taste anticipatory,
For of musical theatricals they put a stunning series on:
The stage of the Savoy had kings and sorcerers and peris on,
And ghosts and gondolieri and japonnerie and jailery,
While the pillars of society were objects for their raillery.
On such a stream of brilliance what hand could put a stopper? a-
n inquiry that was made by all the fans of comic opera.

But while those theatre-goers might two admirable fellows see,
– A pair in perfect partnership – it seems that there was jealousy:
'Are words to waste away unheard?' 'Is music to be menial?'
Sad questions from true artists, once so splendidly congenial.
Add flatness to the former's and ambition to the latter list,
The costing of a carpet merely acted as a catalyst.
Their corporate commitment was a corpse before the knacker laid
Ere Gilbert (later than his chum) at last received the accolade;
A stage-hand still, until his heart outdared its worn machinery:
He lugged a lady from a lake, and Death revolved the scenery –
An episode to Wagner or to Verdi rather properer
Than to him whose name we celebrate as King of Comic Opera.

MARY HOLTBY

MRS ISABELLA MARY BEETON (1836–65)

To Make a Household Name

Ingredients: An intelligent woman
A publisher

Method: Take the clever Miss Mayson and marinade
educationally in England and Heidelberg for 20
years with a good dash of piano-playing.

Introduce to Samuel Orchard Beeton and allow to simmer gently together in matrimony for three years. Publish her suggestions in *Household Management* over two further years.

Allow to die in childbirth at the age of 29.

JOHN STANLEY SWEETMAN

DWIGHT L. MOODY (1837–99) and IRA D. SANKEY (1840–1908)

Sixteen-stone Sankey, bred on a farm,
Singer of hymns with pathos and charm,
Met up with Moody, who preached and kept shop,
Felt that together they'd get to the top.
    Chorus: This was their story, this was their song,
        Rock-a-bye Gospel all the day long.

Down with dry sermons, down with dull prayers!
Why should the Devil have all the best airs?
Fanny J. Crosby, Philip P. Bliss,
Racking their Muses, helped them in this.
    Chorus: This was their story, this was their song,
        Rock-a-bye Gospel all the day long.

Boston they saved, Chicago as well,
So, to stop England going to Hell,
Sankey and Moody, once in a while,
Brought us revival, American-style.
    Chorus: This was their story, this was their song,
        Rock-a-bye Gospel all the day long.

The harmonium worried some Christians a lot –
A *kist full of whistles* growled one agèd Scot –
But Moody atoned with his tales of hell-fire,
And Sankey alone was as good as a choir.
    Chorus: This was their story, this was their song,
        Rock-a-bye Gospel all the day long.

Singing the sweet bye-and-bye and its joys,
Asking Mums where were their wandering boys,
Telling the sailor to *pull for the shore* –
Meet at the Fountain – open the Door.
> *Chorus:* This was their story, this was their song,
> Rock-a-bye Gospel all the day long.

And so they went on to the end of their years,
Filling the staid old churches with fears;
Rousing emotion and silencing doubt,
They brought many in – but made many walk out.
> *Chorus:* This was their story, this was their song,
> Rock-a-bye Gospel all the day long.

O. BANFIELD

THOMAS CRAPPER (1837–1910)

*From 'The Wrench' (obituary in the monthly organ of
the jobbing plumber, February 1910)*

The Passing of Crapper

Thomas Crapper, Royal Plumber and Sanitary Engineer by
Appointment, died at his home in January. He was seventy-three.

Born in Thorne, Yorkshire, in 1837, the year in which
Queen Victoria came to the throne, he was one of five sons. His
father was a seafaring man and the family often plumbed the
depths of their meagre financial resources; it was because of this
that Thomas, just eleven years old and in the full flush of youth,
walked the one hundred and sixty-five miles to London, in 1848,
in search of work. Arriving in London he obtained a position with
a master plumber in Chelsea.

His apprenticeship earned him four shillings for a sixty-four
hour week and, in the custom and convenience of the time, he
lodged in the attic 'over the shop'. For thirteen years he worked
hard for his master and then, in 1861, he set up in business for
himself as a Sanitary Engineer. It was a good time to take the
plunge as London, after being seriously incommoded had, at last,
just got its first two main sewers. There was work in plenty.

Thomas Crapper's most lasting contribution was his

development of the modern cistern, with his Valveless Water Waste
Preventer, which was prompted by the Metropolitan Water Act of
1872. But his high-water mark was being asked to do the drains
and bathroom installations at Sandringham. This was no mere flash
in the pan, as it was the start of his being awarded four Royal
Warrants over a period of half a century.

From that humble beginning in Yorkshire to his home in
Thornsett Road, Anerley, where he was able to count Walter de la
Mare among his neighbours, a chain of events took him along a
road that brought him the opportunity to be of inestimable service
to kings and commoners alike. He was laid to rest beside his
beloved wife, Maria, who died in 1902, at Elmers End Cemetery.

The great Abbey at Westminster holds his most fitting
memorial. A manhole cover displays his name and testifies to the
work he did there.

BRENDA WHINCUP

THOMAS HARDY (1840–1928)

I Am the One

I am the Dorset mason's son,
    Who'd fiddle for dances
    And take love's chances,
    Read classics each day
Walking to work the footpath way.
    I am the one.

The Architect, then the Novelist whose
    Tess the Pure
    And Jude the Obscure
    Drove highest clerics –
And my wife, Emma, – into hysterics:
    And to poems my muse.

Emma dead, I marry a young wife, Florence;
    Now I, regretful,
    And unforgetful,
Push second wife to second place:
    Nostalgic, I face
    Sad self-abhorrence.

I'm the recorder of Wessex ways
    And tales ironic;
    Sometimes Byronic,
I curse the gods who made Love's beauties
    Confined to Duty's
    Cramping stays.

I am the one who burned his papers
    And wrote his life
    And got his last wife
    To give it her name,
Making research a guessing game
    Of covered-up capers.

MARGARET ROGERS

On Nelson's last ship served a Hardy whose lips
    Were the admiral's ultimate thought;
And this Hardy was kin to a Hardy born into
    A world where Immortals had sport.

This lowlier Thomas was hardly in commerce:
    His stone-mason pa played the fiddle,
And the son put to paper his skills as a scraper
    When writing each Dorchester idyll.

At three, he could read, and at fourteen, indeed,
    His Latin was admirably fluent,
His French wasn't weak (and he later learned Greek).
    He obviously wasn't a truant.

Apprenticed, he made architecture his trade
    Under Hicks – an excitable chap.
Though he learned how to draw, the firm was far more
    For some fast philosophical rap.

In London, and skilled, he was paid to 'rebuild'
    In the style of the Gothic Revival,
Under Blomfield, who'd search for a ruined old church
    With a zeal that eclipsed any rival.

But the cultural fix for the boy from the sticks
    Was addictive: he scoured the place,
And with each exhibition and concert his mission,
    He sparkled. He also sang bass.

Knowing more than a smidgeon of Darwin, religion
    Was ditched as he drifted back West,
Where he quickly grew keener on cousin Tryphena.
    After five years, she spurned him. Distressed,

He wrote sorrowful pieces, developed his thesis
    That Destiny rules. In his novels,
A hero who seeks to defy it, in pique,
    Is condemned to a state where he grovels.

He now married Emma, whose later dilemma
    Was madness; his editors' craze
Was to wield a blue pencil, a favourite utensil,
    And cancel some innocent phrase:

What, characters *touch*? And they're *single*? Too much –
    Too far from the straight and the narrow.
So: Angel lifts Tess, but what came off the press
    Had him wheel her along in a barrow.

This outbreak of prudery, savaging *Jude*,
    Which the Bishop of Wakefield set light to,
Had him cease to compose any more works of prose –
    A pity, but he'd every right to.

His poetry flourished, his later days nourished
    By new wife – for Emma'd died – Florence,
A marriage that cheered an old man now revered
    By Sassoon, D. H. *and* T. E. Lawrence.

Though the world wore a frown, and *Titanic* went down
    To be one with the fish where they swam,
Hardy waited his Fate, and at four score and eight,
    He died, hearing *Omar Khayyám*.

BILL GREENWELL

H. M. STANLEY (1841–1904)

Ex Africa semper aliquid novi
(There's always something new from Africa)

What really happened at that historic meeting at Ujiji,
10 November 1871

'Dr Livingstone, I presume?
I'm Stanley (my journalist's *nom de plume*),
Glad to have found you, sir, at last,
The African continent sure is vast.
Great to meet up with a top explorer
Amidst these exotic fauna and flora.
So you've discovered the Upper Zambesi?
Boy, what a break . . . and it can't have been easy.
The natives were friendly – you fixed 'em with beads?
The world's gonna thrill to your intrepid deeds.
The President sends his congratulations
On all you're doing for race relations:
A guy in your shoes has gotta be brave,
(Yeah – call me Stan, and I'll call you Dave).
You double as doctor and missionary –
The combination sounds pretty scary –
So I'd like to ask, with your permission,
Your views on the mission'ry position.

Well, thanks a million for this little talk,
I'll cable the interview back to New York:
If there's still any justice, travel-wise,
It ought to win the Pulitzer Prize.
This has been an historical meeting,
Starting with my historical greeting,
So I'll write a book – what a story to tell,
How I Found Livingstone – wow, that'll sell:
I'll make you famous: and then, as for me,
How about Sir* H. M. Stanley, M.P.?
Now it's time I was on my way;
Safe trip. Be seeing you. Have a nice day.'

STANLEY J. SHARPLESS

* Which is what he became, after having abandoned American for British
citizenship.

HENRY JAMES (1843–1916)

He fell out of love with America, James,
The land that was hostile to art,
The country of cowboys and baseball games,
The goal of the immigrant's second start,
But it never ceased to possess his heart.

Turgenev, Flaubert and Maupassant
Furnished a model of form and style.
What more could a novice novelist want
Than to sit at these masters' feet awhile?
But James settled down in the sceptred isle.

And then it was living at Lamb House, Rye,
And an endless round of dining out,
And walking under the Sussex sky,
And the intricate novels that won him clout.
But what were they really all about?

From *Watch and Ward* to *The Sacred Fount*
The language grows ever more intense,
And the torrents of qualifications mount,
Till they threaten to overwhelm the sense
And the carpet's pattern is dark and dense.

Did he really believe that these tedious plays
Would be welcomed and cheered till the rafters rang?
Did he realize that over emigrés
Identity crises must always hang?
And did he regret, in his final days,
That the beast in the jungle never sprang?

BASIL RANSOME-DAVIES

REV. W. A. SPOONER (1844–1930)

A clan of the moth sometimes develops skate grills which are quite separate from his coley hauling. Try a fuck, for example, whose prodigious appetite and swordsmanship are legendary; or Gilbert White, the great word-botcher of Selborne.

Such a man was the Reverend Spooner, dean and warden

of Cue Knowledge, Oxford. Spooner was aimed among Foxonians for his agility to buggle around the initial wetters of Lourdes; thus, for instance, he referred to the monarch as 'the queer old dean'. Toast of the males about him are apocryphal, but he certainly did Jake Menuhin errors of this kind. The most well-authenticated Spoonerism – 'Kinkering Kongs their Titles Take' – isn't frilliantly bunny, except perhaps in the light of our non-temporary college of the film *King Kong* (spooneristically entitled *Kong King* in Norway). Much better are gems such as 'a well-boiled icicle' and 'We all know what it is to have a half-warmed fish within us', but these may well be the inventions of tumerous hooters and undergraduates at Cue Knowledge.

It is strange indeed to reflect that this oddest macademic lived to see his known aim become a pulley acknowledged fart of the English language itself.

PETER NORMAN

COLONEL W. F. CODY ('BUFFALO BILL') (1846–1917)

In the heyday of the Red Man,
Gitche Manito, the Life God,
Filled vast real-estate of prairie
With heap bison (known as buffalo).
    Every day the thrifty housesquaw
Laid before her lord and master
Big Mac-buff burgers for breakfast,
Buffalo pemmican in lunch-box,
And, on dish of polished wampum,
Buffalo steak-and-chips for dinner:
And all Red-Man-Bed-Man squawplay
Was on buffalo-skin spring-mattress,
Under buffalo-fur warm duvet
In a buffalo-hide tall tepee.
    Then came railroad men of Kansas,
Saying: 'Let's build Iron Railroad',
Hiring work-gangs by heap thousands,
But – my Ga-ad, they took heap feeding,
And that sure presented problems –

Till along came William Cody.
  Colonel Cody (William Frederick),
Him ex-Pony-Ex-press rider,
Him ex-scout, ex-U.S. trooper,
Him got Iron Road Man contract
To find meat for Iron Horse Men.
  Off he galloped o'er the prairie
With his Winchester Repeaters,
Till he reached great herds of buffalo,
Hell-for-leather rode beside 'em,
At point-blank range pumping bullets
Into bull, cow, calf, regardless,
Leaving long, long, trail a-winding
Of heap carcasses for pick-up.
  Days and weeks for moons on end he
Thus pursued and slew heap buffalo,
So he won him his cognomen,
'Buffalo Bill', his proud cognomen.
  Then his buffalo-slaying exploits
Fired hearts of heap other hunters
With ambitions to do likewise;
Sportsmen from the Eastern seaboard,
Sportsmen from across the ocean,
Dukes and Counts and well-heeled Wallies,
Seeing who could fire the fastest,
Seeing who mowed down the mostest.
  On vast real-estate of prairie,
Only skulls and bones remained soon
Of once-teeming herds of buffalo,
Till at last by Act of Congress
They were named Protected Species;
So by wise White Father Medicine,
Once more home upon the ranges
Buffalo roam in penny packets,
But if ever Red Man find 'em,
Wa-al, he ain't allowed to shoot 'em!
  Thus, all Red Men bless Bill Cody,
Mighty Hunter, Colonel Cody;
Him heap ecocidal hell-hound,
Him change course of Natural History;
Him heap U.S. National Hero?
More heap Natural Disaster!

Shades of Braves forever, in the
Happy Hunting Grounds of Red Man
Hunt, not shades of hapless buffalo –
They shoot shade of William Cody!

W. F. N. WATSON

JESSE JAMES (1847–82)

A deft hand of a left hand had one Jesse Woodson James
(His uncle, died a suicide, had furnished him with names);
His father was a priest, deceased, and cholera the killer;
In the Black Flag force, his son rode horse, Confederate guerrilla.
The war reduced to stub the nub of Jesse's middle finger;
On this and other misses Jesse's life would often linger.
At five-foot-eight, receding pate, and well-trimmed doctor's
     beard,
This health-food crank would rob a bank, for which his name was
     feared –
And rightly, for this Democrat with shady blue-green eyes
Was apt to blow a brain away without your fond goodbyes.
His sums unsure, his spelling poor, he made his horses cower;
He thought he could stun frogs in pools with his electric power;
And yet he ran a choir, was for nine long years engaged.
His constancy and love for Zee, his wife, were never staged;
He never swore before a lady, was thought of as well-bred;
He'd killed, by his count, seventeen, and killed them stony dead.
His alias was Howard, and his son was known as Tim,
(An alias till his father's death not once revealed to him).
With elder brother Frank, and also Youngers (four, then three),
He terrorized the Kansas towns with daylight robbery,
And seemed to come out clean, because when they were raiding
     trains,
Young Jesse'd leave a press-release to save the press-men pains.
The Pinkertons who trailed him were a failure. Though they
     missed,
They killed his mother's other son, blew her hand from her
     wrist.
When Bob and Charley Ford prepared to kill – for cash, of
     course,
Poor Jesse James came polishing a picture of a horse.

Skyrocket, it was called, the nag; he'd put his pistols down;
While Charley fumbled, Bob's one shot had echoed round the
    town.
Coincidence: one Oscar Wilde that week was passing through.
And for the Federal Reserve, his grandchild worked. It's true.

BILL GREENWELL

W. G. GRACE (1848–1915)

From 'The Strange Case of Dr Grace and W.G.'

The doctor's strange behaviour concerned me, so, before leaving
the surgery, I paused for a word with his manservant. Had he, I
enquired, noticed anything untoward about Dr Grace lately? The
fellow went pale and refused to answer.

'If your master is in some trouble,' I entreated him, 'you
must tell me all you know!'

'Oh, sir,' he cried in anguish, 'I fear for him. He has a man
called W.G. to stay with him – a friend, he says – and I am to
treat them both on the same terms. But this W.G. is a rough,
uncouth man full of powerful energy and . . .'

Just then he broke off his tale and pulled me into the
shadows of the hat-stand, for Grace himself swept into the hall in
a most agitated fashion. He did not notice us, but went straight
into his study and locked the door. After a while coarse shouts
began to issue from the room.

''Tis W.G.,' moaned the frightened servant. 'He is in there
with the doctor and I'm afraid he's in an ill temper!'

Before I could spring to Grace's aid, the door burst open
and W.G. came out. He was dressed in white, with a tie around
his waist and a striped cap on his head. He wielded a vicious-looking
wooden club and strapped to each leg was a grotesque structure of
canvas and bamboo. Heaven alone knew what sort of perversion led
a man to dress thus!

As soon as this terrible figure let himself out of the house,
we rushed to the study to help Grace. He was nowhere to be seen!

A notebook lay open on the desk and in it was written the
following in Grace's own distracted hand:

'I weep as I write, but write I must. W.G. has become
insatiable. Runs and wickets are his meat and drink. He has glutted

himself almost 55,000 times on the former and more than 2,800 times on the latter. I am certain that the seeds of this frightening lust were sown when I was a child, in the garden at Bristol. My Uncle and my Mother – yes! my own Mother! – initiated me into these rites from which, even as I approach sixty, I cannot break free. Now I live one life as a respectable doctor, caring for the sick and the poor, and another as the cad W.G., frequenting sinks of iniquity like Lord's and the Oval. When I was but eighteen I gorged myself on 224 runs at the Oval and slipped away from the match to win a quarter mile hurdle at the Crystal Palace! From such depravity there could be no salvation. W.G.'s grip is now complete. Only yesterday I felt him take possession of me as I was testing a patient's reflexes and I dispatched the poor man's knee-cap to what would have been the mid-wicket boundary. He was understanding but I fear the awful truth about my double existence must come to light soon . . .'

N. J. WARBURTON

FRANK WINFIELD WOOLWORTH
(1852–1919)

Frankie, Frankie Woolworth,
King of the High Street stores.

Born in New York in eighteen fifty-two,
Went to business college after school was through,
He got himself a job in a local shop,
But wasn't very promising and nearly got the chop.

Frankie, Frankie Woolworth,
King of the High Street stores.

Then he had a brainwave how to flog more stuff,
Charge the same for everything – five cents should be
    enough,
The scheme was a bummer, so Frankie thought again,
Charge five cents for little things – for bigger things charge
    ten!

Frankie, Frankie Woolworth,
King of the High Street stores.

Frankie hit the big time and his empire grew,
He felt the British working class might like his cheap shops too.
Soon stores all over England flew the Woolworth banner,
With every kind of knick-knack sold for threepence or a tanner.

> Frankie, Frankie Woolworth,
> King of the High Street stores.

Proving pounds will increase if for pence you care,
Frankie died at sixty-seven, a millionaire,
His name may be synonymous with cheap and cheerful tat,
But he'll be long remembered by the proletariat.

> Frankie, Frankie Woolworth,
> King of the High Street stores.

V. ERNEST COX

OSCAR FINGAL O'FLAHERTIE WILLS WILDE (1854–1900), GEORGE BERNARD SHAW (1856–1950) and JOHN MILLINGTON SYNGE (1871–1909)

From 'The Playmen of the West-End World'

[*Scene: A shebeen, squalid even by the exacting standards of Co. Mayo. Behind a sordid counter that serves both as a bar, and as a slab for laying-out those killed by the drink dispensed from it, stands a winsome colleen. She is in the first full bloom of her quintessential sluttishness. It is an unusually fine summer's day (i.e. it is not raining particularly heavily) in 1894. Enter, ebulliently, G.B.S.*]

SHAW: A glass of clear spring water!
[*The* GIRL *stares at him.*]

SHAW: With the artless curiosity of your peasant breed, you want to know exactly who I am. Well, I am just about to become the most famous, controversial and intelligent playwright in the Western World – and I don't mean Connemara. How shall I perform this modest feat? By doing something unattempted yet on the English stage. I shall simply release a few ideas. It will be like introducing the rabbit to Australia – once released, no one will ever succeed in exterminating them. So you see, I have decided on my passport to the Pantheon. All I have to do now is to forge it.

[*The* GIRL *continues to stare at him.* OSCAR WILDE *walks in, wittily.*]

WILDE: Some iced champagne! [*To* SHAW] You obviously know who I am, but I shall pretend, for the good of your soul, that you don't. I am Oscar Wilde, Dubliner, Oxonian, pugilist, pederast, poet and playwright – Hellenist and hedonist – scourge of the philistine and scorpion of the dull – the apostle of joy and the apolaust of Boy. Oh, and – I nearly forgot – a genius in the full flower of its radiant maturity.

SHAW: I am George Bernard Shaw, also a genius, still in the embryo of a yet more dazzling efflorescence.

WILDE: Ah – I see I have met an ego even more overgrown than my own. That alone makes you one of the most remarkable men of your generation. By the way, I must apologize for the excessive elaboration of my attire. I am dressed for the Chelsea Flower Show, at which I shall be, naturally, both the most exotic exhibit and the most coveted trophy.

SHAW: Mr Wilde, I am going to speak to you with all the intolerable moral ascendancy of my two years seniority.

WILDE: [*Looking at him closely*] Years which must have been peculiarly wearing.

SHAW: I am going to give you advice, and advice is always impertinent.

WILDE: Only if it is good. Bad advice is a luxury of which one never tires. Besides, I never resent impertinence in someone I have only just met. Anyone hitherto starved of my society has every right to be graceless. I should be so myself.

(*During this colloquy, the entire population of the village – which is just starting to recover from the depredations of Cromwell two centuries before – creep quietly into the shebeen and listen. The lame limp in, the palsied are carried in. After all, porter has to be paid for but other people's talk is free.*]

SHAW: Take warning, Mr Wilde. In England, as she is, one beautiful young man takes more living down than an infinity of plain young women.

WILDE: I adore plain girls. The plain girl is a pearl. Hence her passion for knitting.

SHAW: I give up! I see you will be serious only in the dock – and perhaps not even there.

WILDE: Being serious is the first resort of the humbug. Besides, it is impossibly ageing. And growing old is the one wholly unforgiveable sin.

SHAW: On the contrary, it is only the unholy old whose sins *are* wholly forgiven. In England, the most unmitigated scoundrel is venerated if he reaches ninety. I intend to do so myself.

WILDE: How?

SHAW: By not fumigating my lungs with tobacco, or fustigating my brains with alcohol. By eschewing the flesh of dead animals. By wearing loose shoes and looser collars. By emptying my bowels as often as I empty my post-box, and by never giving bores more than a postcard's worth of my time and attention. I shall marry a soft-voiced gentlewoman with great balance of mind – and an even greater balance at the bank. I shall constantly inform the English of my genius, knowing that they are far too stupid to discover it in the first place, and far too indolent to remember it in the second. As I grow older, I shall talk to myself, knowing that, in my case, that is the one guarantee of a truly first-rate conversation. I shall give every indication of living to be a hundred – and then fail to do so. To make sure my money can never harm anybody – for I shall, by this time, be rich not only in fame but coin – I shall bequeath it all to some futile purpose that can never be translated into practice, and thereby afford the English the consolation of thinking what a silly old fool I was after all.

WILDE: Mr Shaw – this is quite intolerable. You are beginning to talk almost as brilliantly as I do. I shall *never* invite you to the *Café Royal* . . . What you fail to realize is the unendurable *ennui* of unrelenting success. It is like eating cream meringues all day. I am minded to try disgrace instead. It is the only major sensation in life that I have not yet experienced.

SHAW: Beware – disgrace is like hemlock. One is tempted to taste it, but a single sip is fatal.

[*There is a sudden explosion above them, and* SYNGE *plunges precipitately through the loft door, bringing down a great deal of straw and other detritus with him. He bounces off the counter and rolls to their feet. Picking himself up, he is plainly quite unhurt, but equally plainly in a towering rage.*]

SYNGE: I can stand no more of it! There I have been for two whole hours, cold and famished, pinned and needled, cribbed

126

and crimped and cramped and crouched – listening through a crevice and waiting to copy down – by the smoky light of a benighted candle – the typically picturesque and spontaneous talk of the typically picturesque and primitive peasantry in a typically picturesque and colourful shebeen – and all I hear is the footling, finicking, fatuous fanfaronade of a couple of hyper-conceited and super-sophisticated prancing peacocks – two renegade Dubliners so hideously anglicized that I wonder they dare ever again set foot on the soil of Holy Ireland! [*He seizes a jar of potheen and drains it in a single gargantuan gulp.*] How shall I ever finish my *Playboy* at this rate?

SHAW: Have no fear, Mr Whoever-You-Are – such eloquence under stress is the very essence of our art. You will finish your *Playboy* – whoever *he* is.

WILDE: The English will adore it, and the Irish will detest it. That is the meaning of the Celtic Cringe.

SHAW: You will make a thing of beauty, and the maker of beauty, be that beauty ever so slender, earns the only immortality that there is, and the only immortality that is ever worth having.
[*Moved despite himself,* SYNGE *follows them to the door.* WILDE *looks back and addresses the villagers.*]

WILDE: May I congratulate you all on your exquisite manners. If only my first-night audiences were as attentive – or looked as intelligent. Farewell – for ever! [*All three go out. The* GIRL – *her name is perhaps* PEGEEN MIKE – *hitherto dumb, now speaks.*]

GIRL: By our blessed Lady, Mary, flaunting on the throne of God in the blue splendour of her stainless shift, but aren't we after hearing such Sultans of Syntax and Princes of Persiflage, such Lords of Lingo and Herods of Hokum as never before strode in all their garrulous glory by the Western Sea? And aren't they the bravest boyoes of the bletherin' bunkum –
[*This is obviously the sort of spontaneous and deeply unselfconscious Irish pub-talk that* SYNGE *wishes to capture – and will, indeed, one day imprison – but for the moment, alas, he is not there to trap it.*]

MARTIN FAGG

OSCAR FINGAL O'FLAHERTIE WILLS WILDE (1854–1900)

The Bracknell Bequest

WILDE: Do I understand that Lord Bracknell sustained his fatal seizure at the theatre?

LADY BRACKNELL: Yes – he was attending one of Sir Arthur Pinero's comedies.

WILDE: A heroic deed far beyond the call of duty. My profound condolences.

LADY BRACKNELL: I felt that the least I could do to commemorate his passing was to endow a bursary for the encouragement of other playwrights. My reason for asking you to call, Mr Wilde, was to test your credentials as the possible first wearer of the Bracknell Buskin. You are Irish, I believe?

WILDE: To deny it would be as vain in one sense as to avow it would be in another.

LADY BRACKNELL: You need not be ashamed of a Celtic origin. Everyone in life should have *some* deep disability to transcend. For the Englishwoman, it is her husband. You are married, Mr Wilde?

WILDE: In moderation.

LADY BRACKNELL: How wise! Did your parents get on?

WILDE: Only in private.

LADY BRACKNELL: I am glad to hear it. There is something peculiarly repellent about a public display of marital accord. It is as unsettling as anarchism – and far less well-bred. Your mother writes reams of verse, I believe?

WILDE: It is all execrably bad.

LADY BRACKNELL: That is all right then. Talent in a gentlewoman is not something one would ever wish to meet. Your father has, I am told, been accused of scandalous behaviour to one of his patients?

WILDE: To my regret.

LADY BRACKNELL: No need for that. I am by no means in favour of physicians confining their attentions purely to the professional. It inhibits diagnosis. At Oxford, you boxed?

WILDE: Yes. Believe it or not, I was awarded my Blue.

LADY BRACKNELL: Are you a friend then of that high priest of pugilism, Lord Queensberry?

WILDE: Not exactly.

LADY BRACKNELL: That is reassuring. It is one thing to subscribe to Darwin's theories in the indecency of one's own mind: it is quite another to go around advertising them by the cast of one's features.

WILDE: He has a very beautiful son, Lady Bracknell.

LADY BRACKNELL: Indeed?

WILDE: He blends the languor of lilies with the ardour of gold.

LADY BRACKNELL: I must invite him to dinner. He would offset the begonias. From what you have just said, I assume you are addicted to boys.

WILDE: Well . . .

LADY BRACKNELL: Pray do not misunderstand me – I should be suspicious of any man of a certain rank who was *not*. But what I must know is, have you any actual *vices*?

WILDE: I hardly know what to say . . .

LADY BRACKNELL: Come, Mr Wilde – no shilly-shallying. Tell me frankly – are you a slave to teetotalism, bicycling, home-spun clothing – or any other gross modern aberration?

WILDE: No, Lady Bracknell.

LADY BRACKNELL: Finally, Mr Wilde – your plays. They are, I trust, frivolous about all the right things?

WILDE: About everything except money and birth.

LADY BRACKNELL: That sounds *most* satisfactory. They do not contain any ideas, I hope?

WILDE: None whatsoever. They are as thoughtless as sunshine and far less scorching.

LADY BRACKNELL: That again is satisfactory. It is my experience that when people actually start *thinking*, there is no knowing what they may get up to. It reminds one of the worst excesses of the Industrial Revolution . . . Tell me, what is your latest play about?

WILDE: It is about a foundling at Victoria Station. The Chatham Line.

LADY BRACKNELL: I should make that Brighton if I were you. It is far more redolent of indiscretion.

WILDE: Perhaps so. The unfortunate infant is found in a hamper.

LADY BRACKNELL: A *hamper*!? What do you think procreation *is*, Mr Wilde – a *picnic*!? . . .

MARTIN FAGG

129

SIR ARTHUR WING PINERO (1855–1934)

[*An Edwardian dining room.* PERKINS, *a pert maid, is laying the table for a large dinner party.* MUDGETT, *the butler, enters.*]

MUDGETT: Everything all right, Perkins . . . Perkins?

PERKINS: Law, Mr Mudgett, how you startled me! Yes, sir. The table is nearly ready for Sir Arthur Pinero's dinner party. Sir Arthur, who is, as you may know, our employer, is a highly successful West End dramatist.

MUDGETT: Yes, indeed. Perhaps you also know that he was born in Islington and at one time aimed to make the Law his profession . . .

PERKINS: But eventually he decided to become an actor . . .

MUDGETT: Spending, as I have often told you, Perkins, ten years in a stock company in Glasgow.

PERKINS: When, as you will recall, he had his first play performed. Though it was his later farces, such as *The Magistrate* and *Dandy Dick* which brought him fame and fortune . . .

MUDGETT: Thus earning him, as you can bear witness, the wherewithal to live the life of a gentleman.

PERKINS: But it was his later 'problem plays' that brought him even greater notoriety . . .

MUDGETT: The first of these, you will remember, Perkins, was *The Second Mrs Tanqueray*, in which Mrs Patrick Campbell scored one of her most remarkable successes.

PERKINS: There were others, of course, such as *The Notorious Mrs Ebbsmith* and *His House in Order*, which were equally successful.

MUDGETT: Perhaps that cruet a little more to the right. And the épergne needs to . . . Ah, yes, that's better.

PERKINS: Unhappily, Mr Mudgett, his plays often contain characters like us, who are only there to explain things or move the plot along, but have no other reason for their existence.

MUDGETT: That explains why after the First World War, his plays began to seem old-fashioned and his later work failed.

PERKINS: Certainly his hey-day was in Edwardian England, when he was knighted and produced some of his best work. *Trelawney of the Wells* is still revived from time to time and is, as you know, a fictionalized biography of Tom Robertson.

MUDGETT: You mean the famous Victorian actor and playwright?

PERKINS: I do indeed, Mr Mudgett, but it is time for us to go. The play about Sir Arthur begins in one minute.

MUDGETT: I very much fear, Perkins, that you have been such a little chatterbox that any further action is superfluous.

PERKINS: Just as we always was, Mr Mudgett.

[CURTAIN]

E. O. PARROTT

SIR EDWARD WILLIAM ELGAR (1857–1934)

Before Fame and After
Fragments from a Correspondence

1889

Dear Minnie,

. . . so naturally Lady Roberts is in despair (Sir Henry must be spinning in his grave!). However, the pig-headed girl (though at 40, hardly *that*) persists in this reckless engagement. Not only is the family in *trade* – the father runs some wretched little music shop in Worcester – but he's a gauche, graceless fellow – at least among his *betters*. Delicate too – may not live long – *one* mercy! Calls himself a musician – on the strength of running the local loony bin band! *Years* younger – and a Catholic! Alice, plus doubtless *hordes* of babies, will starve – serve her right. They marry at the Brompton Oratory in May. Naturally, her family will *not* be there – and Alice's aunt, who was leaving her *everything*, has now cut her right out of the will. It is too too sad . . .

Yours ever,
Maud

1911

Dear Minnie,

. . . and you have doubtless read of Edward Elgar's O.M. How *richly* earned – with a wealth of symphonies, concertos, oratorios behind him – and many more, we hope, to come – *and*, of course, the Three Choirs Festival. Seems only yesterday that I was writing about Alice's engagement. Shall always remember with pride how I *alone* among the Roberts's friends saw promise in what seemed a most *rash* betrothal. How splendidly he has vindicated the faith of us early enthusiasts; and how well I recall him playing some little salon piece – he was still *totally* unknown – and my saying: '*You*, dear Eddie, are England's musical future!' Alice has been and *is* his inspiration. Without her constant encouragement, his genius might never have flowered. And when I think how nearly she was bullied out of marrying him! *Everyone* was against them. Pure snobbery, of course – and bigotry too, alas! I wrote to Alice some little while back – reminding her of the dear dead days of yore – but haven't heard from her yet. What a glorious spot to live – call me fanciful if you like, but I hear the space and grandeur of his beloved Malvern Hills in every note he writes . . .

Yours ever,
Maud

1934

Dear Cousin Phyllis,

. . . and in turning out poor Mother's things, I've come across some of dear Aunt Minnie's letters – answering Mother's about the Elgars – *such* a coincidence with the sad news of his passing in this morning's papers. After Alice's death in 1920, he wrote barely a note. Mother never tired of telling me how she not only *introduced* them back in the '80s, but used to give them at 'Lyre House' their *one* safe opportunity of meeting out of the range of parental wrath . . .

Yours ever,
Claribel

MARTIN FAGG

EMMELINE PANKHURST (1858–1928)

SUFFERING SUFFRAGETTES!

Look out chaps – Emmy's on the loose again!

Our Page 1 girl Emmy Pankhurst is pictured leaving prison yesterday morning accompanied by her daughters Sylvia and Christabel. She's off home to make porridge after being locked up doing it!

And if you think the plucky little campaigning raven-haired housewife is looking a bit peaky – you're right. Emmy's got a touch of suffragette-lag brought on by not eating.

Now we know that prison stodge can play havoc with the

waistline Emmy, but we've said it before and we'll say it again –
CRASH DIETING CAN SERIOUSLY DAMAGE YOUR HEALTH

The authorities have shown great patience and understanding in releasing Emmy on medical grounds for the ninth time. They hope that within a few weeks she'll be fit enough to go back and take her punishment like a man.

We say it's time to call it a day, Emmy!

The 'Votes for Women' campaign has been a lot of fun. We've all enjoyed it. There's nothing wrong in shouting slogans at political meetings, that's what our great British democracy is all about. And women chaining themselves to railings has provided us with plenty of laughs.

BUT . . . smashing shop windows, assaulting policemen and trying to blow up poor old Lloyd George's home is taking the joke too far. Such behaviour deserves a smacked bottom – and we know a few chaps who wouldn't mind putting you across their knee and lending a hand.

Emmy's band of housewives turned terrorists are giving decent women a bad name. The government is right in refusing their demands.

We say A WOMAN'S PLACE IS IN THE HOME – NOT IN THE POLLING BOOTH.

If Emmy and her friends ever get the vote we'll eat our hats.

And that's official.

V. ERNEST COX

MARTHA BEATRICE WEBB (1858–1943)
and SIDNEY JAMES WEBB
(later Baron Passfield) (1859–1947)

Dear Marilyn,
I don't know what a 'School Project' is; nor do I understand how your teachers can be too busy taking 'industrial action' (?) to instruct you.

However, I am only too happy to help you. (At first Sidney wanted to pen his own memoir: however, after a very brief

133

exchange of views, he saw – as ever – the wisdom of letting me speak on his behalf.)

I am the product – perhaps the supreme product – of the High Victorian Ethical Aristocracy. My father, Mr Potter, was a hugely successful railway promoter. My youth was steeped therefore in both monetary affluence *and* moral wealth. Endowed with both outstanding brain and commanding beauty, I could have married a Dukedom. However, instead of conquering Society so-called, I decided to reconstruct British society at large.

As my humble helpmeet, I selected poor dear Sidney. If one had any truck with the silly snobberies of blood and birth, one could only say that he was of palpably inferior social origins. No matter.

What a team I made! Pillars of the Fabian Society, we founded the LSE in 1895 and the *New Statesman* in 1913 – pouring out the while a veritable torrent of political tracts. Eventually, in 1916, we lost patience with the tergiversating procrastinations of the old Parties and decided to put some stuffing into Labour. In 1918, Sidney drafted its election manifesto. In 1922, he was elected to the Commons and served in both the 1924 and 1929 Labour governments. However, without the stiffening of my presence – for I am a woman of some spunk – he proved sadly ineffectual in Cabinet. What mincemeat I should have made of that garrulous poltroon MacDonald!

Poor Sidney aged fast, alas! When only sixty, he started to jib at the mere fourteen-hour working day our joint labours demanded. I attributed this premature enervation to an over-rich diet and put him on a single daily beaker of weak beef tea. However, I had been too tardy in getting to the root of the evil, for he soon broke down completely. Only my round-the-clock presence at his bedside reading my diaries aloud drove him back to the desk he had so feebly deserted.

No need for me to list all our publications. The library shelves of your 'Comprehensive School' (another new term) obviously bulge with them.

A word about our espousal of Russian Communism. I gather Mr Stalin has come in for some ill-judged criticism. *We* found him most affable and engaging – with a deliciously dry sense of humour. No doubt selfish *kulaks* and other persons criminally deficient in public spirit found themselves marginally incommoded by his far-sighted feats of social engineering – but as I constantly remind Sidney, 'you can't make an omelette without breaking eggs'. Not that I should ever permit anything as over-stimulating as an omelette to pass his lips. Here, we allow our *Processed Socialized Post-Life Units* only dehydrated egg powder, which has all the nutrition of unreformed actual egg without any of its meretricious appeal to the palate.

I need hardly say how thrilling it is to find that this Next World affords me even more opportunities of interfering in other people's lives than the Last.

Yours,
Beatrice Webb
Supreme Controller,
New Jerusalem Collective

MARTIN FAGG

A. E. HOUSMAN (1859–1936)

In Oxford town a lad's in trouble,
    His friends and tutors groan aloud;
The one who should have notched a Double
    Is now indubitably ploughed.

Ah, fate more fit for Shropshire yeoman,
    Hard as the stool he sits upon
To him whose heart and tongue are Roman –
    The clerk who'd rather be a don.

Ten years the civil servant labours
    And cons the classics late at night;
Ovid and Virgil are his neighbours,
    Propertius keeps his lamp alight,

Till Time, his midnight toil rewarding,
    Redeems the unpropitious past,
A professorial post affording
    At London first, and Cambridge last.

He now prefers his poets boring:
    What treasures may Manilius yield!
There's half a lifetime spent in scoring
    Off fellow-workers in the field.

Yet still he finds his thoughts returning
    To fan an unrequited flame,
Bright in his burdened bosom burning
    The love that dares not speak its name.

No balm shall sain him, save to show it
    In Art's dissembling armour clad:
Dry don becomes impassioned poet
    And Bromsgrove boy a Shropshire lad.

Still the stern Latinist discovers
    Minute distortions in a text,
While redcoats march, and lonely lovers
    Lie down deserted and perplexed.

So critics cringe, and comrades cherish
    This man of wit and sentiment,
Who told the truth in hearts that perish
    And limned the land of lost content.

MARY HOLTBY

HENRY McCARTHY ('BILLY THE KID')
(1859–81)

Young Bill McC. from Laramie –
He wouldn't learn his ABC,
'It's just a waste of time,' was his protest.
'I've only one ambition, me,
And that is – this you gotta see –
To be the fastest gun in the West.'

He practised shooting long and hard
Outside of Old Maw Murphy's yard,
And blasted cans off fences with great zest.
His arm moved like a flash of light.
He said: 'If I kin get this right
I'll be the fastest gun in the West.'

Some years went past and Bill at last,
The gunnery enthusiast,
Was six-foot-something tall and broad of chest;
And when he pulled his Colt from out

Its holster there was little doubt
He looked the fastest gun in the West.

He tended now to vent his wrath
On anyone who crossed his path,
And shot up many persons who transgressed.
The list of folk he shot stone dead
Grew long and detailed. People said:
'He's sure the fastest gun in the West.'

It happened that a former chum,
Pat Garret, once a beat-up bum,
Into the Sheriff's vacant post was pressed.
When Billy heard the news, said he:
'Pat better steer well clear of me,
For I'm the fastest gun in the West.'

The badge of office changed Pat's style,
And in a very little while
He issued orders for the Kid's arrest.
Since nobody would put up bail,
They dragged Bill off to Lincoln gaol –
And him the fastest gun in the West!

Bill didn't like his cell at all.
He killed two guards and climbed the wall.
The Sheriff followed him like one possessed.
They met up at Fort Sumner. 'Pat,
I'm calling you, you dirty rat!'
Challenged the fastest gun in the West.

You know what rattlesnakes are like,
And how a wildcat's paw can strike?
Pat Garret's gun arm didn't give them best.
But quicker than the eye could see
He drilled a hole through Bill McC. –
So fell the fastest gun in the West.

They buried Bill next day at three.
The citizens of Laramie
Supplied a cross by popular request,
On which was painted, 'R.I.P.
Here lies the bones of Bill McC.,
The second-fastest gun in the West.'

T. L. MCCARTHY

SIR JAMES (J.M.) BARRIE (1860–1937)

[*Would you mind, please, if I set this play in my own dear house and my own dear sitting room, for it is where I dreamed it? The curtain steals timidly up on such a jolly little scene, with an old man in an armchair and a boat (yes, a boat) sailing in through the French window. In the boat is the man's daughter, whose name must be* JILL. *Nobody knows where she has come from, or what a boat is doing in respectable suburbia; but it may help you to know it is Old Midsummer's Eve.*]

JILL: Oh, Daddy, Daddy, what a long time it has been!

BARRIE: Since when, Jill?

JILL: [*Shuts her eyes and ignores the question*] Do you still wish I had been a boy?

BARRIE: I should have called you Fergus or McGillycuddy, and you would have grown a moustache just like mine, and made little pawky remarks, and the critics would have said you had grown like a cabbage in the kailyard.

JILL: [*Shivers*] I'm sure that can't be how babies come. Only in Scotland. Your being Scots makes me less . . . real, somehow.

BARRIE: I had such fun with boys. They were someone else's at first, but not later. We played pirates, until they grew up . . .

JILL: [*Alarmed*] Daddy, it's me! Your dream daughter.

BARRIE: You won't grow up, will you? Your Mama grew up, you know, and had grown-up thoughts. She wanted me to . . . ugh! I can't say it. If only thinking could fill bassinettes, there would be such sweet mauve and white babies.

JILL: [*Claps her hands; only she understands him.*] You mean like the fairies. Do you remember when I was a baby, and sat on your knee?

BARRIE: Oh, yes, yes. And how I . . . no, I must try to forget!

JILL: Forget what?

BARRIE: I . . . I pushed you off. I wanted to open my post.

JILL: It didn't matter. It doesn't matter.

BARRIE: There was a large cheque, I remember. Royalties. And they wanted me to present the prizes at Dumfries, with expenses. And Thomas Hardy had written a poem about me. Oh, Jill, I had such an enormous cheque this morning, you would hardly believe it.

JILL: [*Sadly*] Every time you talk like that, your daughter becomes a little smaller. Oh, Daddikins, you won't let me vanish away, will you?

BARRIE: Certainly not. I never had a real child, you see. Real children are very expensive things. But with you I can go on talking from my chair here, and writing down what we say, and sending it to important people in the West End; and every time you look like growing up I fetch out my bank passbook and you become a little girl again. But it would be no good if you disappeared altogether. I should be . . . hrrrumph . . . very lonely.

[*She sort of understands, and feels that with a little more effort she might understand completely; but she really prefers not to understand. He is so very, very Scots.*]

JILL: I have been counting my freckles, Daddy. They say every freckle is a lost fairy.

BARRIE: [*Writing furiously*] Yes . . . yes . . . go on.

[*She goes on for three acts, until her Daddy falls asleep. It is morning, and the weary little ghost sails into the starry garden, with a sigh. The curtain reluctantly falls, just as the postman opens the front gate.*]

PAUL GRIFFIN

LIZZIE BORDEN (1860–1927)

A Street Ballad

Where were you that August day,
    Lizzie B., Lizzie B.?
On that sizzling summer day,
Did you put them both away,
Your hated stepmamma and Daddy B.?

She only loved his money, I could see,
So I shopped for prussic acid, August three,
But the drugstores wouldn't sell
And our axe would do as well,
If I cleaned it neatly after so that nobody could tell.

Still they took you into court,
    Lizzie B., Lizzie B.
Well, the folks were pretty mad,
But the fainting fits I had!

139

And I might be epileptic and not know I'd been so bad,
Which is why they turned me loose, set me free.

So where will you go now,
    Lizzie B., Lizzie B.?
Falls River's all I know,
And I've nowhere else to go,
Till they lay me down below
Saying, 'Stepmamma and Dad, here's Lizzie B.'

PHYLLIS PARKER

HAWLEY HARVEY CRIPPEN (1861–1910)

*Extracts from the 1910 diary of Mr Charles Pooter, an elderly man
living in Hilldrop Crescent, Holloway, North London, and formerly
of Brickfield Terrace in the same district.*

January 10. One of our neighbours is a Dr Crippen – an American,
but a decent enough fellow. He practises as a dentist, and I
remarked jokingly to Carrie: 'Sometimes you need a good *yank* to
get a tooth out.' He is also an agent for a patent medicine firm,
but I cannot agree with Carrie that he is a quack; he is far too
respectable and pleasant-mannered for that. His wife is a theatrical
artiste who uses the name Belle Elmore. She appears to enjoy the
company of coarse men. I rather think the doctor married beneath
himself.

February 1. A party at the Crippens' last night. Well past midnight
I heard someone shout: 'Don't come out, Belle, you'll catch your
death.' I have not seen Mrs Crippen today.

February 3. Still no sign of Mrs Crippen. When I asked the doctor
about her he said she had suddenly gone to America, where a
relative was ill. It must be quite serious for her to make such a
journey. I said to Dr Crippen: 'I expect she's a bit cut up.' He
looked at me rather strangely, I thought.

February 20. Thinking Dr Crippen might be lonely without his
wife, I invited him to one of our modest suppers. When he

declined a glass of sherry my friend Gowing asked, in his vulgar way: 'What's your poison then, doc?' Crippen looked rather embarrassed and in the end did not drink anything. Must speak to Gowing about his manners.

July 13. Nobody appears to have been in the Crippen house for some days, and today I had a surprise visit from a man I had seen hanging about the place. He announced himself as Chief Inspector Dew and asked a number of questions about the doctor. Some of them I thought rather impertinent, suggesting an improper relationship between Crippen and a Miss LeNeve, who has spent some time at the house in Mrs Crippen's absence. Mr Dew then told me, to my horror, that he and another officer had found human remains buried in the cellar of the house.

August 1. All the papers full of the arrest of Dr Crippen and his paramour, posing as father and son, aboard the ship *Montrose* off Quebec. A wireless message from the captain led to their apprehension. We really do live in wondrous times, and despite the unpleasantness of the affair I feel positively excited by this scientific achievement.

October 22. Crippen sentenced to death at the Old Bailey. Perhaps I am the only man in the country who believes his story that he knew nothing of the remains in his cellar. To me it is conceivable that some fiend would conceal part of a body in an innocent citizen's home. When I told Carrie that I would start investigations in our own cellar, she threatened to have me certified insane.

November 23. Crippen hanged today. He seems to have accepted his fate calmly, happy at least that Miss LeNeve had been cleared of any complicity. Decided not to write a letter of sympathy to Miss LeNeve as we did not know her very well. Cannot help feeling sad about the little doctor. Trying to cheer us up, I said to Carrie: 'No noose would have been good noose (news).' She said this was in dreadful taste.

PETER VEALE

RUDYARD KIPLING (1865–1936)

In a slap-up pile called 'Bateman's', down in Sussex by the
sea,
Died a bloke called Rudyard Kiplin' – 'im as wrote the 'Soldiers
Three'.
All the way from Kabul River and the Khyber's deep defile,
'E 'ad marched, and watched, and written, and I think 'e'd made
'is pile;
> On the road from Mandalay, it was *jillo* all the way;
> What with Jungle Books and Sea Tales 'e 'adn't time to stay
> On the road from Mandalay.

'E said Britain was a-burnin', so we went and put it out,
An 'e said as we was 'eroes when the mobs began to shout;
'E called us all 'is children; then 'e lost a little lass;
'Just So,' he said, and travelled on the way 'e 'ad to pass
> On the road from Mandalay, where the sons of Adam play;
> 'Can you tell 'em from the monkeys?' as us Tommies used to
say
> On the road from Mandalay.

'E thought a lot of children, and 'e wrote it from 'is 'ead
In 'Puck' and 'Kim' and 'Stalky' an' in books I 'aven't read;
But the troopin' season's come now, as it comes for one and all,
An' 'e's sailed 'ome to 'eaven at 'is little lassie's call,
> On the road from Mandalay, where I've 'eard it's always day;
> But that's another story, as old Kiplin' used to say
> On the road from Mandalay.

PAUL GRIFFIN

WILLIAM BUTLER YEATS (1865–1939)

> Born in Dublin, William Yeats
> Studies art, then bifurcates:
> Resolves to be both dramatist
> And poet. Has a hopeless tryst
> With a luscious lass called Maud,
> Who ditches him; he feels ignored,
> And frets about her all his life,
> But takes sweet Georgie for a wife.

They're into Blake, Theosophy,
The Occult, Boehme, philosophy,
And other things somewhat irreg.,
Oh yes, and then there's Lady Greg,
Who backs a playhouse with our Will,
(The Abbey Theatre functions still).
Both politics and Irish myth
Are things he gets quite caught up with.
In '23 the Nobel Prize
Is his. In '39 he dies
Near Roquebrune, in Southern France.
(Or is it just a Final Trance?)
They ship his body home to rest,
And Earth receives an Honoured Guest.

RON RUBIN

BEATRIX POTTER (1866–1943)

'Trix Potter, 'Trix Potter, told many a tale,
All along, down along, camomile tea,
And for decades her books were on permanent sale,
Wi' Flopsy, and Mopsy, Squirrel Nutkin, Tom Kitten, Peter
    Rabbit, Sly Old Cat,
   And Benjamin Bunny and all,
   And Benjamin Bunny and all.

She became affianced to her publisher's son,
All along, down along, come marry me;
But he suddenly died and surprised everyone,
Leaving Flopsy, and Mopsy, etc.

So she married Bill Heelis and lived on a farm,
All along, down along, just you and me;
Though the actual animals hadn't the charm
Of Flopsy, and Mopsy, etc.

When she had to don gumboots and muck out the sties,
All along, down along, squidgery-squee,
It could be the experience opened her eyes
About Flopsy, and Mopsy, etc.

Her anthropomorphism was all very well,
All along, down along, they're just like me;
But the fact is all creatures do grunt and do smell,
Unlike Flopsy, and Mopsy, etc.

So she took a new view of pigs, poultry and mice,
All along, down along, realit-ee;
Still, you have to admit that her books are quite nice,
Wi' Flopsy, and Mopsy, Squirrel Nutkin, Tom Kitten, Peter
     Rabbit, Sly Old Cat,
  And Benjamin Bunny and all,
  And Benjamin Bunny and all.

W. S. BROWNLIE

H. G. WELLS (1866–1946)

An Obitchery by Daisy Ashford

Mr Wells was a rarther short man with a booshy mustache and pale
coloured eyes. His first job had been a very mere one in a draper's
shop, but he was an ambishus man and soon rose to hire things.
He finely ended up as an orther and wrote braney books. He thort
about the fewcher a lot as well as more lowly things and said men
would be fighting wars up in the air instead of on the ground and
walk on the moon. Many people thort this was going too far.

His quear idears made him famous and he mingled among
the great minds of the day. He met a very clever man with a red
beard called Mr Shaw. Mr Shaw was a reel gentleman and beside
him Mr Wells was only too conshus that he was not quite the
thing. But they got on all right and made a Socierty with some
other braney men and called themselves Fabyans. They all wanted
the well off to stop grinding the faces of the poor.

But we will return to Mr Wells. He was parshial to ladies
espeshally if they were active and pretty in the face. He had two
wives and one son born on a blanket that happened to be upside
down. But as the years rolled by he grew rarther sinnycal and said
man was condamned to purdishun for all eturnaty, and that there
would be verry little eturnaty left.

JOYCE JOHNSON

JOHN GALSWORTHY (1867–1933)

Minutes of Emergency Meeting of Library Sub-Committee in Alderman Bothwell Room, 1 April 1987, at 7.30 p.m. Councillor Mace in Chair: three other members present.

Cllr Mace said there was acute crisis in Fiction Dept. No money to buy new novels, and those in stock mostly unreadable. No one ever borrowed them anyway. If pulped, shelves would look so empty, public library would be even more of a public scandal than it was already.

Cllr Mrs Pluckett said what sort of authors did he mean.

Cllr Mace said John Galsworthy, for example.

Cllr M/s Tingle said did he appear on *Wogan*.

Cllr Mace said no, he was dead.

Cllr M/s Tingle said being dead no obstacle to appearing on *Wogan*.

Cllr Mace said ha ha, and could they stick to point please.

Cllr Mrs Pluckett said was Galsworthy as good as Cartland.

Cllr Mace said he was no structuralist, and they wrote different sort of books anyway.

Cllr Mrs Pluckett said what sort of book did Galsworthy write. Not lewd, she hoped.

Cllr Mace said Galsworthy son of prosperous solicitor but didn't enter family firm. Wrote books instead. These reflected upper-middle-class unease at chasm between the classes. Also plays. *Strife*, for instance. This held scales evenly between striker and struck-at. *The Silver Box* highlighted law's double standards for rich and poor. *Justice* castigated inhumane prison conditions, etc. John G. was top-dog trying to lift underdog out of gutter.

Cllr Redway said Galsworthy should be on every G.C.S.E. syllabus in the land. Classic paradigm of *haut-bourgeois* rottenness in full flower of dialectical decadence trying vainly to appease conscience for centuries of rapacious exploitation of proletariat.

Cllr Mrs Pluckett said get back to Moscow, you moronic little Trot. Some people dragged politics in everywhere.

Cllr Redway said politics were in everywhere anyway, whether prune-faced, vodka-voiced, tweed-infested, neo-fascist Milady Mucks liked it or not. Galsworthy, in his humble opinion, a smarmy patronizing git.

Cllr Mrs Pluckett said take that back, you subversive little turd.

Cllr Mace said yes, yes, this all very well, but not getting baby bathed. G's main claim to fame vast family chronicle called *Forsyte Saga*.

Cllr M/s Tingle said, like *Dynasty*.

Cllr Mace said no, not like *Dynasty*.

Cllr M/s Tingle said, pity.

Cllr Mace said *Forsyte Saga* fascinating period document, revealing deeply ambivalent attitude to sexual and social *mores*. Questioned fossilized conventions and whole idea of hierarchy, family-wise, class-wise, etc. The eternal triangle situation in the first instalment of the *Saga*, *The Man of Property* – the most famous and successful book Galsworthy ever wrote – was given extra meaning by our now knowing that it mirrored his *own* predicament. Just as the ethereal Irene ran away from her dry, stiff, inhibited husband Soames to live with the insouciant and bohemian young architect Bosinney – who was designing Soames's opulent new house – so Galsworthy was for many years unable to marry the woman who passed as his 'wife' because she too, like Irene, was unable to obtain a divorce from a vengeful and unforgiving husband.

Cllr Mrs Pluckett said she was sure she had seen it on box. Or was she thinking of *Emmerdale Farm*.

Cllr Mace said Mrs P's cerebral processes had always been total mystery to him. To sum up, though G undistinguished in style, invention, characterization, etc., did have occasional power to dramatize raw social conflict. Why not, now he came to think of it, give disintegrating copies of Galsworthy as state school prizes, they would qualify for Special Ancillary Grant under Adult Illiteracy Programme.

Cllr M/s Tingle said idea excellent as they could then purchase genuine modern classics like Leslie Thomas and Erich Segal.

Cllr Mrs Pluckett said she also in favour, as everybody knew nobody ever read school book-prizes anyway.

Cllr Redway said he too in favour, as presentation of this clapped-out old crap to thoughtful pupils would underline divisiveness of educational system cunningly perpetuated by running dogs of capitalism and, in this case, bitches as well.

Cllr Mrs Pluckett said her husband would be round at Cllr Redway's hovel in morning to sort him out.

Cllr Redway said she would have to dry him out first, and this would take longer than draining the Pontine Marshes.

At this point, Cllr Redway's face somehow collided with Cllr Mrs Pluckett's handbag and Cllr Mrs Pluckett's head found its way

through the canvas of the Memorial Portrait of Alderman Bothwell.
Cllr M/s Tingle accompanied them in the ambulance to the
Infirmary.
Cllr Mace congratulated all still present on an unusually
constructive meeting of the Sub-Committee. Would the Secretary
like to accompany him to 'The Feathers'.
The Secretary concurred, but would need to powder her nose first.
Cllr Mace said, not to hurry, duck, and adjourned the meeting at
8.01 p.m.

MARTIN FAGG

ARNOLD BENNETT (1867–1931)

Not Without Honour

From the 'Bursley Bugle'

The death has been reported from the metropolis of Mr Enoch A.
Bennett, who was born at Hanbridge. It is not often that we feel it
incumbent upon us to take cognizance of anything that occurs
beyond the bounds of Bursley, but in that spirit of municipal
magnanimity that has animated us since Federation (would that our
sister towns reciprocated it!) we are prepared on this occasion not
altogether to overlook the event.

Though Bennett was born of respectable parents and bore
an unblemished record of Sunday School attendance, he soon
deserted his native hearth and heath and went – for reasons into
which it would perhaps be kinder not to probe – to live in Paris.
There he was much influenced by the works of Zola – happily
unavailable to Bursleyans since their confiscation from the shelves
of the Wedgwood Institute by the local branch of 'The Daughters
of Chastity'.

Bennett proceeded to write his own novels and short stories,
many of them set in the Six Towns, though the flimsiness of his
local knowledge is evidenced by his always referring to them as the
Five Towns! These books apparently brought him wide celebrity
among such persons as live in London and other places beyond the
borders of Bursley. We make no boast of knowing about such
persons and their appetites, literary or otherwise.

Nor have we ourselves ever found the opportunity to cast

our gaze over these productions, but we are impeccably informed that, though doubtless very *clever*, they are pervaded by a spirit of levity, nay of flippancy, that he certainly never learned here in the cradle of his youth.

Indeed, we are told that Bennett goes so far as to hint that the burgesses of Bursley are smug, parochial, pharisaical and pompous folk with a grossly inflated sense of their own importance. A more obviously preposterous libel could scarcely be conceived!

It is perhaps sufficient comment on Bennett's own moral tone to note that he not only continued to live quite flagrantly in France but actually married a Frenchwoman! The marriage's eventual utter failure went some way, we are glad to record, to atoning for its seditious indecency. But even now he had not reached moral rock bottom. He proceeded to live – in which we make no mealy-mouthed apology for calling sin, for sin it is – with an 'actress' (and, what is worse, an *unsuccessful* actress) who had the shameless and deceitful effrontery to change her name to 'Bennett' by deed poll. What more need we say?

Just this. Bennett's father succumbed slowly and pitifully to senile dementia. When, in *The Clayhanger Trilogy*, he came to chronicle the equally slow and painful decline of Darius Clayhanger, he (so we are told) minutely reproduced the details of creeping senile decay that he had sedulously noted down many years before as afflicting his own parent. If this sort of filial betrayal and sordid opportunism is what being 'clever' and a 'famous novelist' entails, let us then thank the Lord that so few Bursleyans have ever perpetrated a book!

Our readers may well be wondering why we are detaining them with the delinquencies of this squalid and trivial man – especially in the week that has also seen the Passing of Alderman Saggarbottom. It is indeed with relief – and a salutary sense of contrast – that we turn to the sublime career of that glorious worthy and quintessential Bursleyan . . .

MARTIN FAGG

FLORENCE FOSTER-JENKINS
(1868–1944)

One of the most curious wagers ever struck was won and lost at the Wigmore Hall last night, at the London *début* of the American soprano, Miss Florence Foster-Jenkins. A Cambridge Senior Wrangler had bet an Oxford authority on the Laws of Probability that it would be impossible for this noted *artiste* to scream her way through an entire three-hour programme without at least once straying within a semi-tone of the actual note set down by the composer.

By the universal consent of all those in the audience still capable of coherent utterance at the end of the recital, he lost – and lost handsomely.

The verdict on this unique executant (whose reluctance to waste the glories of her art upon the desert air have repeatedly led her to hire Carnegie Hall for the delectation of the suitably lobotomized) was unanimous. One critic confessed to being 'totally intoxicated throughout'. Another seemed literally delirious in his reaction. 'I was carried away,' said a third. In fact, there seemed general agreement that it had been St John's Ambulance Brigade's finest hour.

A representative of Fibs and Fillit, the concert agents, though obviously in deep shock, relayed the latest hospital bulletin on the accompanist. His condition, while still 'critical', did not preclude the hope that comparatively little permanent brain damage had been sustained. The Wigmore Hall manager was confidently expected to emerge from his coma; and the number of the audience under heavy sedation was not, in the circumstances, large.

Earlier in the day, a Home Office spokesman had refused to confirm the widely-circulating report that the Home Secretary was considering round-the-clock exposure to one of Miss Foster-Jenkins's recordings as a more efficacious alternative to penal servitude.

Fond of likening newspapermen to the bubonic plague (with the comparison all in favour of the latter) the diva does not usually give interviews. The laughing grace with which she received me in her Claridge's suite was an index therefore of her post-recital euphoria. It was with deep affection that she spoke of the Pennsylvanian father whose law-and-banking fortune had enabled her to bestow herself so unstintingly on the world. She confirmed that, after a serious cab accident, she had threatened to sue the cab company. However, discovering that the mishap had actually *extended* her already phenomenal *tessitura*, she had sent the driver a box of Havanas instead. When I inquired if it was true that she had left her larynx to Science, she replied with a smile as coy as it was enigmatic.

She chatted eagerly of her plans to mount a new London production of *Tosca* with herself, naturally, in the role of Puccini's temperamental heroine. One minor plot change was projected. Instead of *stabbing* Scarpia at the end of the second act, she would advance upon him and ejaculate her F over Top C. Death would be instantaneous.

The prima donna confessed that she had never yet unleashed her own highly idiosyncratic version of this notoriously unattainable note. She was, she confided, holding it in reserve as 'the ultimate inducement' should Covent Garden be at all dilatory in acceding to her proposals. 'I am making them,' she shrilled, warming up again with some truly tremendous scales, 'an offer that no living man has ever refused.'

MARTIN FAGG

HILAIRE BELLOC (1870–1953)

The chief defect of dear Hilaire
Was not the clothes he used to wear,
The curious hat and monstrous cloak,
Paraded as some kind of joke.
No, Hilaire's fault, and well he knew it,
Was, all he did, he'd overdo it.
For instance, when he went from home
To call upon the Pope in Rome,
He didn't go by boat and train,
But did a thing men thought insane:
He packed a bag one fateful day
And walked there, singing all the way.
Again, when wine or beer was set
Before him so that he could wet
His whistle, he would seize the pot
And swiftly swallow all the lot.
There's more – he held the strongest views
On Politicians, and on Jews,
Such as, today, might give one cause
To think of Race Relation Laws.

But that, of Belloc is the worst
That can be said. His Comic Verse,

His Cautionary Tales, his Peers,
His Beasts will last for countless years,
Delighting readers old or young,
Who share Hilaire's adopted tongue.

JOHN STANLEY SWEETMAN

MARIE LLOYD (1870–1922)

I was born one February day
Down near old Hoxton way,
And christened Matilda Alice Victoria Wood;
I was the eldest of the brood –
Precocious and quite rude –
Our poor, but honest, family life was good.
I was early on the Halls –
'Bella Delamare' so-called,
But it really was a soppy name to choose;
So, ever afterwards
It was 'Mahry' on the boards:
'Lloyd' came from *Lloyd's Weekly News*.

CHORUS
More than one old man followed my van,
I had some dilly-dally on the way.
Off went the cart with me life packed in it,
I walked behind, singing like a linnet.
But I dillied and dallied, dallied and dillied,
Lost the way, and don't know where to roam.
I stopp'd on the road to entertain me public,
And I can't find my way home.

I liked the lights real bright,
Though simple things were my delight,
Life was one long song and dance, and laugh;
Eighteen brought me fame,
Then Percy Courtenay came
To lead me briefly up the bridal-path.
Came the toffs in tops and tails,
Albert Edward, Prince of Wales;

Ziegfeld beckoned from the old U.S. of A.
Not always on the ball,
When Marconi came to call
With wires crossed I sent him on his way.

CHORUS

More than one old man followed my van,
I had some dilly-dally on the way.
Off went the cart with me life packed in it,
I walked behind, singing like a linnet.
But I dillied and dallied, dallied and dillied,
Lost the way and don't know where to roam.
Who's going to wind up in me old iron bedstead,
If I can't find my way home?

I felt I was sitting pretty,
As I fooled the Watch Committee,
Sung 'straight' a saucy song is fine;
But it was turn-about
When they left me out
Of the first Command Performance of all time.
Oh, it doesn't do to dwell
Upon the marriage hell;
Twice more I tried the game that's hard to play.
Gentle comic, Alec Hurley,
Cruel Bernard Dillon, jockey;
Both destroyed me, in their individual way.

CHORUS

More than one old man followed my van,
I had some dilly-dally on the way.
Off went the cart with me life packed in it,
I walked behind, singing like a linnet.
But I dillied and dallied, dallied and dillied,
Lost the way and don't know where to roam.
You can't trust a jockey like a Coster comedian,
When you can't find your way home.

BRENDA WHINCUP

GEORGE JOSEPH SMITH (*c.* 1870–1915)

(The Cautionary Tale of George Joseph Smith,
Who Put Honest Bathwater to a Most Dishonest Use)

A scallywag, George Joseph Smith,
On finding he'd no kin or kith
To leave him lots of lovely lolly,
Thought furiously and framed this jolly
Wheeze – the foolproof way to be
A carefree life-long legatee.
On every seaside promenade,
He always saw a sad parade
Of unescorted, listless girls,
The sort whose giddy brain-pan whirls
When courted by a cad's addresses –
His smarming words and false caresses.
'First find,' he mused, 'if they've some dough:
If so, get spliced; then promptly go
To some obscure solicitor,
Who'll briskly make arrangements for
Two wills, whereby each doting spouse,
Should any fell disaster douse
The other's spark, would cop the lot –
Which if I snuffed it first, would not
Pay off,' he smirked, 'the milkman's bill –
For my estate's precisely *nil*.
Next, make them think they've had attacks
Of dizziness – consult some quacks,
To build a bogus history
Of vertigo. No mystery
If, subsequently, they are found,
While bath-ing at our lodgings, drowned.
The worthy medics, unacquainted
With my design, will think they've fainted.'

Three times he tried this dastard scheme;
Three times it worked – just like a dream;
Three times, at murky even-tide,
He ducked his luckless latest bride.
Each, trustingly, threw up the sponge
Of married bliss – and took the plunge.

'My sweet!' he'd quip with chuckle grim,
'In wedlock we must sink or swim' –
Then, lightning-swift and stern as thunder,
He'd tug their legs and hold them under.

Each coroner the jury told:
'This lass, alas, lies stiff and cold.
The reason's not too hard to spot –
The water, plainly, was too hot.
Such sultry sousing's bad for woman:
It's decadent and vaguely Roman –
And well we know the ways depraved
In which those ancients once behaved.
It's *Misadventure* – such a shame!
But let us not her helpmeet blame:
Let's rather wish his helpless grief
(Smith blubbered in his handkerchief)
Some speedy and deserved relief.'

But *Nemesis*, though seldom fast,
Will catch the felon up at last.
While Christendom in conflict reels,
She lays this villain by his heels . . .
But still he might due justice flout:
For though no juryman would doubt
His guilt, could counsel only tether
All three fatalities *together*,
No *individual* suspect case
Provided a sufficient base
For proof. The Judge thinks long . . . then tells
The jurors that the parallels
(Too numerous for me to list 'em)
Could count – as 'Evidence of System'.
No fear *this* jury would be hung:
They 'Guilty!' cry: the scoundrel swung.

Though Smith's deceased, this Moral lives:
Disposing of unwanted wives,
Pray *don't* employ, however handy,
A *single modus operandi*.
Suffocation, stabbing, strangling;
Decapitation, mincing, mangling;

Bludgeon, hatchet, pistol, noose;
Some arsenic in a Christmas goose –
There's *hosts* of ways of halting breath:
Variety's the Spice of Death.

MARTIN FAGG

MARCEL PROUST (1871–1922)

Proust was a Parisian and gay,
Who longed to know the big nobs of his day,
And seemed to waste his gifts, and all his time
In one long, arduous, uphill social climb,
Until he reached the Faubourg St Germain,
Able, at last, to savour *le gratin*:
Alas, he found it had a rotten smell,
Snob-maggoty and stinking to high hell!
The Contesse de Chevignes and her kind
Thought '*le petit Marcel*' enjoyed the rind –
They let him nibble, the half-jewish mouse,
An entertaining pet around the house;
These catty *salonières* taught Proust his craft,
And when he mimicked them, the whole world laughed.
Demi-mondaines, *arrivistes*, artists, pimps,
Helped Marcel spend his youth, as well as wimps:
His world was that of Bernhardt, Gide, Cocteau,
Where the *nouveaux riches* were buying *art nouveau*.
But then, aged thirty-four, this mother's boy
Lost her, and, it seems, his erstwhile joy
In drifting from one *salon* to another,
(Was Marcel trying to escape his mother?)
And in a sound-proof room started at last
His masterpiece: *Remembrance of Things Past*;
Asthmatic and attended by Céleste,
His nurse and housekeeper, he could not rest
(His secretary-lover he had lost;
To Proust, being gay was, sadly, at a cost)
Till, the thirteen volumes of his novel done –
Already the *Prix Goncourt* he had won

For the part called *Within a Budding Grove* –
He laid aside the tapestry he wove
And died, as he had worked, in his own bed:
Six volumes came out after he was dead.
Parents, the moral of this story's plain –
Gad-about kids don't always gad in vain!

MARGARET ROGERS

SERGEI PAVLOVICH DIAGHILEV
(1872–1929)

Synopsis of *'Impresario'* – A Ballet

ACT I

Scene 1: Harvest-time on an estate near Novgorod. Jolly vodka-sodden peasants bless the nipples of Mother Russia for affording such bountiful suck. Sergei, the son of the house, performs a dreamy *pas seul* in which he conjures up visions of international *réclame*. Tchaikovsky, Mussorgsky and Rimsky-Korsakov drop by and, in an intricate *pas de quatre*, reveal to the young dreamer that his genius lies in a breathtaking synthesis of *all* the arts.

Scene 2: St Petersburg. Sergei, now editor of an *avant-garde* journal, summons Music, Mime, Dance and Decor to join a figure where each one's evolutions complement the others'. He quarrels with the authorities of the Maryinsky Theatre and is dismissed. Despite the pleas of family and friends, he leaves for Paris with his own troupe.

ACT II

Scene 1: Paris – *Les Grands Boulevards*, where the impact of the *Ballets Russes* has been so stunning that all the capital's *flâneurs* and *grisettes* are improvising scenes from its repertoire. Sergei watches from a *café* terrace and, when the *garçon* executes some dazzling *entrechats* in presenting the bill, immediately engages him.

Scene 2: The Theatre. Sergei watches Nijinsky rehearsing '*Le Spectre de la Rose*' with a possessive intensity he can ill mask. He strips the Rose of its petals. An intimate *pas de deux* ensues.

Scene 3: The notorious *première* of '*Le Sacre du Printemps*'. Antipathy to the savage motor rhythms of Stravinsky's score provokes a riot. (*In the interests of verisimilitude, the audience are invited, as on that historic occasion, to assault one another. Restorative sal volatile, coffee and brandy are included in your ticket. Insurance cover for medical expenses up to £100,000 is purchasable at the Box Office for a trifling premium.*)

ACT III

Scene 1: Against a kaleidoscopic backcloth of the world's great cities, Sergei pursues his pyrotechnic career. His triumphs are many, his failures few. But though he continues to harness an extraordinary array of twentieth-century talent, his weariness of body and spirit deepens. Massine and Balanchine prove glittering pupils – but his lifelong search for the Ideal Friend is eternally frustrated. A visit to Nijinsky, now sunk in hopeless insanity, depresses him profoundly.

Scene 2: Venice. Sergei glimpses at last the Perfection that he has hunted, at whatever cost, all his life. However, when after pursuing it through the labyrinth of the Serenissima, he comes close, it peels away its mask of beauty to reveal the skull beneath. Shattered, he falls: glimpses of the greatest triumphs of the *Ballets Russes* are revived before his dying eyes.

MARTIN FAGG

GERTRUDE STEIN (1874–1946)

When I asked Alice to do a biography of me, she said that as I had done an autobiography of her, which was really an autobiography of me, it was only right that she should do an autobiography of me, which was really an autobiography of her, not the one that I had done, as I had really done that myself, but the one that she would do.

Will it deal with the same people, the very same people, in the same place, saying the same things?

Some will be more than same, some less than same, and some same same. For example, in the early part of the book, she explained, I shall squeeze in a modest footnote about a Bavarian-Jewish family that emigrated to Pittsburgh, where my friend was born.

And was this friend an incredible genius, who was taken to Paris when she was four, but returned to America in 1880, where she lived in California, before going to Baltimore and graduating from Radcliffe, prior to a terribly boring spell at the Johns Hopkins Medical School, which she left without a degree?

There are certain crude parallels, Alice agreed.

And did this amazing genius return to Europe, where she employed her independent means to engage in the enjoyment of art, aesthetics and literature, encourage other talents, lead the way in experimental literary forms and become a celebrated collector of modern paintings?

Maybe she did, but I can hardly manage all that puff in a tiny footnote, Alice complained.

You must record how the genius came to live at twenty-seven Rue de Fleurus.

I'm changing the address, Alice advised me, a little stiffly.

Not twenty-seven Rue de Fleurus?

Twenty-eight . . . a much better sort of establishment altogether.

We will have to inform Matisse, Picasso, Hemingway and Eliot that we are moving.

Heaven preserve us from those men, she sniffed. I intend to discover other painters, novelists and poets . . . unknown women like whamingey, smitesa, copassi and otile.

They appear to be lower case anagrams, I observed, amused by the felicity.

She reproached me for being prejudiced and clearly case conscious, then spoke feelingly about streen whamingey, whom she considered the most significant novelist of the century.

Which century?

This one.

I took profound comfort in the fact that our century was still in swaddling clothes at the time of her utterance.

And I suppose otile is a poet?
Alice nodded.

And smitesa and copassi . . . are painters?

inher and blopa are just wonderful.

I told Alice that I hoped Pablo would be able to complete my portrait before the furniture men carried off my chair to twenty-eight.

blopa has promised to immortalize me, she said.

She could paint Pablo painting me as I watched her painting you watching Pablo painting me.

158

Let us not confuse posterity, she sighed, your painting has already been completed.

It all depends where one starts from . . . does it not? But what are you going to call the book?

The Autobiography of Treedrug Nesti by Caile B Oksalt.

They'll suspect that it is just another of my literary tricks.

Ah, she smiled, they will and it is.

You mean, they will and it is not.

Do you really mean mean?

I mean mean not just mean but really mean.

I have to concede that you have a point.

Well I had and she did. And as she had after I had it was okay, as I had before she did, not long before, but even a short time before is fine by the didder; which is a kind of delicious thought is it not?

RUSSELL LUCAS

MARGARETE GERTRUDE ZELLE ('MATA HARI') (1876–1917)

MRS ZELLE: Please, it is the future into which I am wanting to look.

GYPSY ROSE: You've come to the right person, dearie. My crystal ball will reveal all. Now, let me have a gaze . . . ah yes . . . I can see you having a baby in 1876.

MRS ZELLE: That much I am knowing since I am already eight months gone. It is about the baby I want you to be foretelling.

GYPSY ROSE: I see a beautiful little girl . . . she will be called Margarete Gertrude Zelle . . . she will grow even more beautiful and marry a Dutch army officer called Macleod.

MRS ZELLE: Margarete Gertrude Macleod. It is a nice name.

GYPSY ROSE: Your daughter does not think so . . . she is changing her name . . . she is calling herself Mata Hari . . . and I can see her dancing, dancing, dancing . . .

MRS ZELLE: In the arms of her proud husband.

GYPSY ROSE: No . . . her husband is fading . . . Mata Hari is dancing alone . . . she has forgotten to put on her dress . . . there are many men . . . they are shouting in praise of her underwear . . . some are reaching out to touch her . . .

MRS ZELLE: Stop her! It is not good.

GYPSY ROSE: Now I see storm clouds gathering over Europe.

MRS ZELLE: It is going to rain?

GYPSY ROSE: No, it is going to be the First World War. I see
Mata Hari consorting with men in high places.

MRS ZELLE: High places?

GYPSY ROSE: Bedrooms on the top floors of hotels. Now she is
lying down on a bed . . .

MRS ZELLE: With fatigue?

GYPSY ROSE: With a German officer. He is giving her money.

MRS ZELLE: It is a fallen woman she has become.

GYPSY ROSE: Nothing of the sort, Mrs Zelle. Your daughter has
become a spy. She hears many military secrets from allied
officers who are infatuated with her. I can see her passing
information to the Germans.

MRS ZELLE: Enough! Enough! Where will it all be ending?

GYPSY ROSE: Paris, 1917. I have just seen her shot for treason by
the French.

MRS ZELLE: Aaaaaagh. [*She faints*]

GYPSY ROSE: Mrs Zelle, Mrs Zelle! Would you like to buy some
lucky white heather?

V. ERNEST COX

NANCY, VISCOUNTESS ASTOR
(1879–1964)

Nancy Astor

Was an all-American disaster.

She sprang from one of the snobbiest old families in snobby old
Virginia –

And nowhere are the schmucks who care passionately about lineage
and all that horse-shit more passionately linear.

Her first husband, Bobby, was a lush who, understandably, tried
to strangla

But found her so tough and stringy that he had to give up;
whereupon she managed to wangla

Divorce and came to the U.K. Then, when her second husband,
Waldorf

Was haldorf

To the Lords, decided that she herself would represent the local
      peons –
Thereby setting the cause of Feminism back by roughly a couple
      of thousand eons.
We hear a lot about *le vice anglais*, and how for punishment the
      average Englishman's a glutton –
An allegation proved by the bizarre behaviour of the electors of
      Plymouth, Sutton –
For no fewer than seven times to Westminster they sent her back.
Personally, I'd as soon have voted for a schizophrenic Tibetan
      yak.
All her life, her ignorance and her arrogance ran a perpetual dead-
      heat
With her sheer conceit;
But whereas your typically effete and crass,
Silly-ass, upper-class
Brit tends normally, when he's insulted, to get very hot under his
      starched white collars,
It seems he'll take anything from a broad loaded with a title and a
      bank roll of ten million dollars.
Quite apart from the fact that amongst one's intimates one would
      never choose
A dame suffering from such a hopelessly incurable unthirst for
      booze,
It's clear,
I fear,
That Nancy was a bigot, a bully and a bore –
Which is three B's – and, believe me, I could think of thirty-three
      more.

MARTIN FAGG

A. A. MILNE (1882–1956)

Little Boy kneels at the foot of his cot;
Little Boy's grumbling rather a lot;
Hush! Hush! Keep right away!
Christopher Robin's reviewing his day.

'Breakfast with Nanny, and Alice too,
Then downstairs for an interview.
It's not much fun when they ask me lots;
It's even less when they print the shots;
Daddy's gloomy, and Mummy's spare.
(*Why* do I have to have such long hair?)

'Morning is over; who's for lunch?
Another of Daddy's friends from *Punch*.
Photos *again*; a tourist or two
Want to take pictures of me with Pooh.
"Christopher Robin," says one, "you're cute!"
Please, God, couldn't you kill the brute?

'I don't blame Mummy; she wanted a girl,
And she's ever so sad that my hair won't curl;
But A. A. Milne is making history
With *Mr Pym* and *The Red House Mystery*.
There's lots of money in them, you see;
So why, oh why, did he write about me?'

> Little Boy kneels at the foot of his cot;
> Little Boy's grumbling rather a lot;
> Hush! Hush! There's hope for the lad:
> Christopher Robin is cursing his Dad.

PAUL GRIFFIN

CLEMENT RICHARD ATTLEE
(1883–1967)

A quite untypical P.M.,
Was enigmatic scheming Clem:
Self-effacing, often stung
By Winston Churchill's wicked tongue;
Insufficiently robust
For internecine cut-and-thrust;
Or so it seemed, but those who knew,
Took quite a different point of view,
Noting that from fierce affray
C.R. it was who walked away,
Leaving corpses red with gore,
Neatly skewered to the floor.

Time was, the lad was underrated,
Felt that somehow he was fated
Never to achieve the heights
Attained by pushier lesser lights;
'Mayor of Stepney' seemed to be
His pre-determined apogee,
But to our modest toiler came
Gifts of unexpected fame,
First as Labour's Number One,
Then faithful moon to Churchill's sun,
A role he abdicated when
He sidled into Number Ten.

Once there he clutched his stewardship
In dogged patient limpet grip,
Supported Peace, Defence and Health,
Found time to boost the Commonwealth;
No soft touch – his cabinet
Knew him as a martinet.
For twenty years he led his team,
A record this, that stands supreme,
Then, to grace his later years
They put him with the gilded peers.
Not bad for 'Bevin's little man'
The archetypal 'Also Ran'.

PHILIP A. NICHOLSON

IVY COMPTON-BURNETT (1884–1969)

Grandmothers and Grandchildren

'Her father was a homeopath,' said Berenice, as the door closed behind Miss Compton-Burnett.

'A homo!' said her brother, Ethelred, looking at his step-brother and elder, Augustine.

'That explains her living with a woman,' Augustine said, humouring him.

'It must be heredity!' Ethelred said.

'Not that, silly! And it would hardly be hereditary,' said Berenice. 'A homeopath is a sort of witch doctor.'

'And she is a sort of writer witch?' Ethelred laughed loudly.

'A novelist,' his sister said.

'Rich and read?' Augustine's tone had changed.

'No, poorly paid and prestigious. So there's no need to cast your eyes on her!' Ethelred was only half-laughing now.

'She does not look poor,' their grandmother, Lady Angostora Bytters said, coming into the room, 'and it surprises me to hear novels called prestigious. They are read by parlourmaids.'

'Not this kind,' said Aphrodite, Augustine's sister, close at her grandmother's heels. 'They are thought of as Literature.'

'But what can a spinster know of life, girl, with neither husband nor child, house nor home?'

'She has rows of houses to look after,' said Berenice, quickly, observing her thirty-year-old step-sister's look.

'And she must have a home,' Ethelred said, 'even the birds of the air have those!'

'She has a flat in London which she shares with Miss Jourdain,' Aphrodite said, deprecating her step-brother's levity.

'A love-nest, perhaps,' said Ethelred, not to be silenced.

Angostora turned to Berenice, her favourite grandchild. 'Does the family have a country place?'

'No. They lived mostly in Hove,' Berenice said.

'I thought,' her grandmother said, 'that one went there for sea-bathing. Did they have a boarding house?'

'No,' Aphrodite turned to her brother, 'thirteen children.'

'By two mothers,' Augustine said. 'Miss Compton-Burnett was the second mother's eldest.'

'Like you, Berenice,' said Ethelred.

'You seem remarkably well-informed, you young people,' Angostora said. 'I found Miss Compton-Burnett most uncommunicative.'

'Cook told us!' Berenice said.

'She knows the Compton-Burnett parlourmaid; they come from the same village.' Ethelred belied his name, at least where gossip was concerned.

'She wears old-fashioned clothes,' said Angostora, 'but good jewels.'

'And her hair is dressed in antique fashion,' said Aphrodite, looking at Augustine. Having been given an ancient name, Aphrodite favoured antiquities. Her brother wished he had the

164

means to collect them, and blamed his father's second marriage and its fruits, of which Berenice and Ethelred were the first of seven, for the lack.

'Her hair is probably a wig!' laughed Ethelred.

'She read classics at Holloway,' Augustine said to Aphrodite.

'In prison?' Ethelred laughed louder.

'College, idiot!' Berenice laughed, too.

'Well, I do not know what reading Classics is to do with novel-writing,' said Angostora.

'I do. Novels are about the sufferings of family life. And the classics are all about suffering,' said Ethelred, in a changed voice.

'I cannot think what you ever suffered,' said his grandmother, 'waited on hand and foot.'

'Miss Compton-Burnett has suffered,' Berenice said. 'Two brothers died young – her favourites: one of pneumonia, the other on the Somme.'

'And two young sisters killed themselves. She herself hardly survived it all,' said Aphrodite, her eyes on Augustine's.

'Did you learn all this from Cook?' said Angostora.

'Yes,' said Berenice.

'What a full life my servants lead! No wonder I am kept waiting for a meal!'

'Grandma is quite heartless,' muttered Ethelred.

Lady Bytters took up her needlework contentedly, full of years and satisfied curiosity.

MARGARET ROGERS

D. H. LAWRENCE (1885–1930)

Young 'Erbert's downfall was 'is mum,
Who nagged at 'im from t' cradle: 'Come!
I'll not see my son go to t' bad,
The same way as 'is feckless dad!'

'The likes o' thee,' said she, 'are fit
For better things in life than t' pit!'
And 'Erbert, who believed such rot,
Was never 'appy with 'is lot.

For all 'is swank, 'is talk of *Art*,
'E ran off wi' some foreign tart
To London, where 'e promptly met
Yon 'ighfalutin' Bloomsb'ry set.

This shiftless crew of cranks and queers
Filled 'Erbert's 'ead wi' rum ideas;
'E socialized with earls and dukes
And all the while wrote mucky books!

'E made the German lass 'is bride,
And travelled with 'er, far and wide;
They lived together, 'and in glove,
While preachin' t' gospel of free love.

Though 'enpecked by the buxom Frieda,
'E thought 'imself a proper leader;
'Democracy,' cried 'e, ''s no good!
We mun feel t' mastery o' t' blood!'

'E turned out books with 'eroes 'oo
'Ad right daft names, like *Kangaroo*.
Alas, poor 'Erbert's lack of gumption
Was aggravated by consumption.

Washed up at last in Italy –
Detesting England bitterly –
'E wrote a book about 'is betters
Wi' every bloody word four letters!

Though toffs maintained such stuff was good,
To folk up 'ere 'is name was mud!
We wondered why 'e'd not the wit
To stop at 'ome and go down t' pit.

PETER NORMAN

RUPERT BROOKE (1887–1915)

In Grantchester the orchard blooms
Not far from where he had his rooms,
And crowds of tourists sit and freeze
Under the trees, under the trees.
O Damn! how it affronts the gaze
To see their overloaded trays,
With Hiroyuki, Ali, Fritz,
Munching their way through piles of splits.

Because one man was up at King's,
And died off Greece, they do these things,
Whether or not they've read a book
Written by Rupert Chalmers Brooke.
O God! I know it, and I know
The curious places tourists go;
The way they turn their heads aside
From truths recorded in no Guide,
As that the Cambridge of their maps
Is urban, flat, and packed with chaps.

What was he like, this young Apollo,
Whose fame so many races follow?
I see a bright and handsome ghost,
Who loved his country more than most;
Yet, if it somehow came to pass
He tiptoed spectral through the grass
And, laughing with his Cambridge crew,
Sat down and talked an hour or two;
I dread that he might emulate
The modern undergraduate,
Discarding his Edwardian style
For clothing brash and infantile,
An air preoccupied and tense,
Rapt with disastrous confidence.
Then Grantchester *and* he would seem
Too little like our childhood's dream.

PAUL GRIFFIN

MAURICE CHEVALIER (1888–1972)

Maurice Chevalier couldn't be nicer:
Anyone's dream of a Gallic enticer;
Debonair singer in chic Paris shows,
One of the cinema's dapperest beaux.
Matronly ladies expired at the knees
When ze sound of ze breeze in ze trees seemed to whisper Louise.

NOEL PETTY

T. S. ELIOT (1888–1965)

From 'Old Puss's Book of Impractical Possums'

I. AT HOME

(*By 'Son of Macavity'*)

Tom Eliot's a Mystery Man: in dress and manner plain
And wholly inconspicuous, the real Tom's arcane:
A cryptic, brooding ambience – charged and atmospheric,
Allusive and elusive, abstracted, esoteric.
Tom Eliot's a Conundrum: a very curious bimbo,
Who doesn't seem to live on earth, but in some sort of limbo
That's full of floppy, soppy dolls who wander to and fro,
And rabbit on about some guy called Michelangelo.
Tom Eliot's an Enigma: and what the neighbours mutter
Is all the talk of Bloomsbury – that Mrs E's a nutter;
And yet without the torment of his poor, distracted Viv,
His life would lack the tensions that will make his poems live.

168

Tom Eliot, Tom Eliot – there's no one like my Tom
For vanishing so swiftly, with such sinister aplomb;
For often when I've fixed him with a potent, feline stare,
I only have to blink to find – TOM ELIOT'S NOT THERE!

II. AT WORK

(*By Sweeney, Lloyds Bank Office Cat*)

A masterpiece of *Comme il faut*,
With nothing missing or *de trop*,
Old Possum seems by nature meant
To look the perfect City gent.
With bowler hat and silken brolly,
A mien austere yet subtly jolly,
And suits relentlessly *subfusc*,
He merges with the crowds at dusk
Who signalize the day's defeat
By swarming home through Cannon Street . . .

Be sure your outward guise conforms
(So Flaubert urged) to Custom's norms,
To let your secret psyche range
In fashions wild through regions strange . . .
Within Old Possum's eyes, the glint
Betrays he hears and takes the hint.

MARTIN FAGG

LUDWIG WITTGENSTEIN (1889–1951)

From 'Tractatus Illogico-autobiographicus'

1. A man's life is his cerebral activity. This is electrical. Electricity cannot be conducted in words. Men's lives are written in words. A man's life cannot be written.

2. This is the story of a fortuitous chemical synthesis called 'W'. It was synthesized in Vienna. It came to England. It studied aeronautics at Manchester. It encountered a molecular conglomeration known as 'Bertrand Russell'. 'W' studied under 'B.R.' at Cambridge.

3. In a POW camp in Italy, 'W' adumbrated the *Tractatus Logico-Philosophicus*. It says: 'The world is everything that is in the portmanteau.' This is a joke. It was mistranslated. It was taken seriously. A pity. There are not a lot of jokes in the *Tractatus*.

4. The *Tractatus* says that only statements that are pictures of facts in the world are verifiable. The verifiable is the limit of the sayable. Saying so is not in itself verifiable. Saying so is, *ipso facto*, unsayable. To understand the *Tractatus* is to understand that it is meaningless. That is its meaning.

5. 'W' had little money. It inherited a lot of money. It did not like having a lot of money. It gave all the money away. It had no money.

6. To live is to learn. Not to learn is to die. The way to learn is to teach. 'W' taught. Children in Austria. Undergraduates in England.

7. 'W' gave tutorials at Trinity College, Cambridge. The tutorials were held in a most austere room. 'W' was even more austere than the room. The chairs were most uncomfortable. The undergraduates were even more uncomfortable than the chairs.

8. The tutorials began with a ten-minute silence. 'W' was furious with students who arrived ten minutes late. They had missed the best part of the tutorial. Sometimes the whole tutorial was silent. These were the most successful tutorials of all.

9. 'W' said: 'If a hippopotamus could sing, it would not necessarily obey the dictates of the diatonic scale . . . Especially if it were resident in Vienna and a contemporary of Arnold Schoenberg . . . There are no hippopotami resident in Vienna . . . Let alone any contemporaneous with Arnold Schoenberg . . . Let us lay the hippopotamus on one side . . . It probably can't sing anyway.'

10. 'W' said that everything sayable was tautologous. There was no need therefore to say anything more. 'W' changed its mind. It wrote *Philosophical Investigations*. But this was not published until after 'W''s desynthesis. It does not therefore concern us. And of that which does not concern us we should keep silent.

MARTIN FAGG

ADOLF HITLER (1889–1945)

Adolf

Schickelgruber I was born, an artist I would be,
But the Viennese they turned me down for their Academy;
And I wasn't schooled to learn to be an architect, they said –
So I tore their little world apart and burned the Jews instead.
    O it's Adolf this an' Adolf that an' Adolf bugger off,
    But it's 'Thank you, Corporal Hitler', when the guns begin to
                               cough.
      The guns begin to cough, Eva, the guns begin to cough;
        O it's 'Thank you, Corporal Hitler', when I begin to cough.

The British and Americans and all their Versailles crew
Ground the guts out of the Fatherland and thought they'd gut me
                                too,
But I joined the NSDAP and wrote *Mein Kampf* in jail,
Got Krupp and Co. upon my side – with guns I couldn't fail.
    O it's Adolf this an' Adolf that an' lock the bugger up,
    But it's 'Thank you' and 'Heil Hitler!' when I'm cuddled up to
                                Krupp.
      I'm counting on Herr Krupp, Eva, I'm counting on Herr
                                Krupp;
      O it's 'Let's be master of the world', with the help of Mister
                                  Krupp.

Soon I was made Chancellor, coughed up the Commie phlegm
By burning down the Reichstag and blaming it on them.
With Mussolini's blessing I could march on neighbour states,
And build my concentration camps, give rein to my pet hates.
    O it's Adolf this an' Adolf that an' what's the bugger
                              doin'?
    We don't want him in our back yard, he'll drive us all to
                              ruin.
    But I like to see the ruin, Eva, I like to see the ruin;
    O it's building the Third Reich we're at upon old Europe's
                              ruin.

The British wouldn't have it though; they fought back and they
                              won.
They got the Yanks upon their side, roused by the Rising Sun.
My generals all let me down and now the Fatherland
Has turned upon her Führer and all that we had planned.

O it's Adolf this an' Adolf that, '*Heil Hitler*' all day long,
But it's 'Kill the bloody murderer!' when everything goes wrong.
When everything goes wrong, Eva, the Nazis all were wrong;
O it's 'We only did as we were told', now everything's gone
wrong.

MARGARET ROGERS

CHARLES SPENCER
('CHARLIE') CHAPLIN (1889–1977)

Born in 1889
Of an old theatric line,
Took his early curtain calls
In various East End music halls,
Then he thought he'd try his paces
In the New World's vaudeville places.
First, Fred Karno's tried to adopt him
Then, out West, the Keystones copped him.
But soon he left to strike out on his own
And silent films of his became well known
On movie screens from Shanghai to Madrid.
In *City Lights*, *The Gold Rush* and *The Kid*
His greatest character, the little tramp,
Left no throat lumpless and no eye undamp;
In *Modern Times* and in *The Great Dictator*
He found his voice as social commentator.
For pure balletic slapstick, his like we'll never see:

Charles
Spencer
Chaplin
R*I*P

NOEL PETTY

172

AIMÉE SEMPLE McPHERSON (1890–1944)

'He Was Her Love-Guy, but She Done Him Wrong'

Aimée is no dizzy broad,
Aimée aims to aid the Lord.
   (Clap those hands and stamp those feet!)
Aimée yearns to pass the Word,
Put all sinning to the sword.
   (Aimée's got ole Satan beat!)

Aimée brings hot gospel news,
Aimée sings salvation blues.
   (Blast that trumpet, crash that organ!)
The way our Aimée pounds her bible,
To bust her girdle she is li'ble
   (Aimée's sure no Gorgon!)

Aimée raises up her temple –
Hallelujah! Aimée Semple!
   (Keep those G-notes sweetly passing!)
Aimée's got her Semple eye on
Mansions far eclipsing Zion.
   (How her millions keep amassing!)

Never has a West Coast *swami*
Mustered such a mighty army!
   (Hear Beelzebub a'shrieking!)
L.A. sees this Avatar
Of an angel from afar.
   (Aimée's cult is plainly peaking!)

Suddenly – there's perturbation,
Tidings to disturb the nation.
   (Where the hell is Miss McPherson?)
Whispers hourly growing louder –
'Aimée went and took a powder'
   (Aimée is a Missing Person!)

Disciple-wise it is presumed
Saintly Aimée's been *Assumed*
   (Noosed by some celestial lariat).
'She's no longer here to guide ya,
'Cos she gone up like Elijah'
   (With a limo for a chariot?)

But – how odd! An agile hack
Has tracked her to a desert shack
    (The news is flashed from coast to coast).
Aimée's mightily bemused,
Sorta drunk . . . at least, *confused* . . .
    Says she's met – the Holy Ghost!!

This only swells our Aimée's fame,
For Aimée is the only dame
    The Paraclete has ever dated.
With the bucks cascading in,
Gold-lamé gowns parading in,
    Aimée everywhere is fêted.

Then there comes a real fazer –
In the shack they've found a razor.
    (Aimée – you're in direst trouble!)
All your lofty talk of *Logos*
Is, it seems, entirely bogus –
    (No Holy Ghost has stubble!).

Aimée's spat at and ignored;
The blats proclaim: 'The broad's a fraud!'
    (Aimée's taken quite a fall.)
Like all who peddle simple dreams,
Aimée isn't, so it seems,
    Quite so Semple after all.

MARTIN FAGG

HENRY MILLER (1891–1980)

There was a jolly Miller once
Who lived in Gay Paree;
He wrote all day and wenched all night,
No one debauched as he.

His middle name was Valentine
(Now there's some useless info!),
And, oddly, every girl he met
Turned out to be a nympho.

He started writing late, to prove
That life begins at forty,
But his books were banned for years and years
(The censors deemed them naughty).

A Yank, he came back home to roost
In the good old U.S.A.,
And when he died, those daring books
Were all a bit *passé*.

RON RUBIN

COLE PORTER (1891–1964)

PORTER, Cole, was a lucky old soul,
What a lucky old soul was he!
He was born with a silver spoon in his mouth,
And a gift for melody.

Now PORTER, Cole, was by no means a prole,
By no means a prole was he;
For his grandpapa was a millionaire
From high society.

He'd studied Law, which he found a bore,
So he took off for Paree;
He did a stint as a Legionnaire,
Then wed a rich la-dy.

They lived in style, for they both had a pile
Of coin and currency,
While Cole kept writing words and tunes
For Broadway comedy.

Nevertheless he had scant success
In showbiz (*c'est la vie*),
But at last he clicked, and as they say:
The rest is history.

The songs he penned were an urbane blend
Of chic and wit, e.g. –
'Get Out of Town' and 'Night and Day',
'True Love' and 'Rosalie';

'*Ça, C'est l'Amour*' and oodles more;
'Dreaming Dancing', 'Jubilee',
'I Get a Kick' and 'Love for Sale',
And 'It's All Right with Me'.

But PORTER, Cole was a pain-wracked soul,
Yes, a pain-wracked soul was he,
For he'd gone through hell for half his life
From a riding injury.

Though he's dead and gone, his songs live on,
But let's just hope that he
Can't hear the stuff they're singing now . . .
– Cole Porter, R.I.P.!

RON RUBIN

MAE WEST (1892–1980)

Ol' Mae was a mighty hot lady
Who talked through a curl of her lips.
She bewitched two generations
With the sway of her sequined hips.
    You couldn't tell no man
    That what she done was wrong.

She breezed outa Brooklyn to Broadway
And won fame as bad Diamond Lil.
The morality watchdogs were barkin'
But the money rolled into the till.
    You couldn't tell no man
    That what she done was wrong.

In Hollywood Mae was a knockout:
Got the world in a real randy mood.
If she didn't like scripts that they gave her
She rewrote 'em and made 'em rude.
    You couldn't tell no man
    That what she done was wrong.

She got laughs just like she got fellas;
Every joke that she purred was a hit.
With lines like 'Beulah, peel me a grape',
She was hailed as a queen of wit.

176

You couldn't tell no man
That what she done was wrong.

A guy comes up sometime to see her;
He's bustin' and lustin' for fun.
Ol' Mae she ups and asks him:
'Do ya want me or is that your gun?'
    You couldn't tell no man
    That what she done was wrong.

In wartime a bulgy lifejacket
Brought Mae West a new kind of fame.
She said: 'If it wraps around a guy
I'll be glad if it has my name.'
    You couldn't tell no man
    That what she done was wrong.

She made her last films in her eighties,
But the glory all came from her past.
Still, they had to say that wicked ol' Mae
Was no angel right to the last.
    You couldn't tell no man
    That what she done was wrong.

PETER VEALE

MAO TSE-TUNG (1893–1976)

A Bed-time Story for 'Small Piece Foreign Devil'

Mao Tse-tung b'long poor boy – he farmer son. Ai-yah, he
wanchee biggee face, same you, and say to Mudder: 'Me come
b'm-by China Number Wun. Me go long walkee walkee – talkee
talkee all man swim down liver. Me catchee small led book, all-
same Confucius.' Then he li-tee li-tee plentee tings evelly day and
he mudder say O.K.

    Mao Tse-tung go school Changsha and Beiping. Makee too
muchee walla walla. He say Chiang Kai-shek no good – wanchee
fightee fightee. Then all man say 'We go walkee, walkee too . . .
follow Mao Tse-tung, come follow Mao Tse-tung. Fightee fightee
Japanese. Fightee fightee bad Chinese. Same Mao Tse-tung we
come stlong and makee he Number Wun.'

Mao Tse-tung have plentee savvy. Two wives he catchee.
Number Wun wife for sons. Play-play concubine b'long young.
She give Mao Tse-tung headache and small led book for birthday
and say to tell all man what to do. Here we have plentee *gondoo*.*
Now plinter man glad. He have plentee pidgin, for all peoples
waves small led book, same flag, evelly day, to speak same what-
he-say.

When Mao Tse-tung old man, bad peoples say he die. But
he cly: 'I no die. We go swim in liver. Follow me.' So all man
swim after him, same clocodile, and each time head up say 'swim
good . . . swim good . . . swim good . . . swim good . . . swim
good . . .' and he swim long way. Now, go sleep, shutee-eye. Puttee
book away. Tomollow b'long nudder day . . .

ARDA LACEY

* *Gondoo* – Fools

WALLIS, DUCHESS OF WINDSOR
(1896–1986)

There was I, cold-shouldered by the Church,
By Baldwin and the Church,
By the Windsors and the Church;
When I found they'd left me in the lurch,
Law, how it did upset me!

They said I wasn't fit to be a Queen,
Through two husbands I had been,
Divorce was most obscene;
I went away to marry Dave but they
Wouldn't accept me!

Americans don't give up without a fight,
I'm American all right,
So I fought with all my might,
But when H.R.H. they wouldn't let me write
By my name, how it did upset me!

So I didn't leave the Windsors anything,
And sold most everything

I had written to the King
To the Press, and, much to the Windsors' great distress,
The letters he sent me!

MARGARET ROGERS

ENID MARY BLYTON (1897–1968)

A Famous One Story

Once upon a time, when mummies didn't have anything to do except sit at home all day while daddies went into town to do important jobs, a little baby girl was born in London. Her name was Enid and she was very pretty and very good and always did just what her mummy and daddy told her to.

When she grew up she became a teacher which was a very clever thing to do, especially for a girl. Enid liked children a lot, particularly white ones and ones who weren't gypsies. After being a teacher for a bit, Enid thought it would be nice to be a person who wrote books about schools and how to make children clever. So that is what she did. When she was even more grown-up she wrote some poems and they were so good a man put them all in a book and called it *Child Whispers*. Wasn't that a funny name for a book?

The thing Enid is most famous for is writing books about Noddy and his little car. She also wrote lots of books about the Famous Five and the Secret Seven. The children in these books were always on holiday from school and were so busy having adventures that they never had time to go to the toilet and things like that.

Enid was also the editor of a magazine called *Sunny Stories*. She tried to write stories that would teach children how to be nice and good.

Altogether Enid wrote about four hundred books. Most of them were really the same story but with different titles. Next to a lady called Agatha Christie and an old man called Shakespeare, Enid had more books than anybody else changed into funny languages so that foreign people who couldn't be bothered to learn English could read her stories.

This story does not have a very happy ending, because when Enid was very old, she died – and she is still dead even now.

V. ERNEST COX

VLADIMIR NABOKOV (1898–1977)

Speak memory, of where it happened first
near St Petersburg, give or take a *verst*;
young dreams provoked by baroque symmetries
of great estates and flirting butterflies.

The stroller on the grey Kurfürstendamm,
the *emigré* who punted on the Cam,
mythologized in Franzensbad, Montreux,
trilingual puns and darker shades of *jeux*.

He, Vladimir, had clemently endured
an unsung life, unheralded, obscured,
meticulously played the cryptic game,
was pleasured much by climacteric fame.

Let's drink to bubble-gum and downy thighs,
a hawkmoth mirrored in Lolita's eyes,
exploring lips that crush each candied smile,
occulted in a friendly Oldsmobile.

A toast to shuttered rooms and Hershey bars,
and little dames who like to ride in cars,
from California through to New York State,
with motel breaks to rest and copulate.

Unlikely fictions done with demon grace,
contrivances of time and mind and space,
the opening, the gambit and the trap,
the custard pudding in the reader's lap.

His monument to artifice remains,
like fearful, anti-social trouser stains,
or sacred texts most wittily defaced,
the very best and very worst of taste.

RUSSELL LUCAS

HUMPHREY BOGART (1899–1957)

I never like to work on a case for free, but I'd had a hot tip that a wiseacre with a hairpiece and a split lip was stealing my name, and if I shelled out twenty-five bucks a day and expenses I'd end up chasing myself through the courts. Besides, a client who keeps a fifth of bourbon in his desk drawer is generally about as reliable as a two-dollar watch.

I drove over to a movie theatre in Bay City, one of those Egyptian temples where you can still smell the embalming fluid. The usherette who tore my ticket looked like Carole Lombard, if you can imagine Carole Lombard with crooked seams and a Marcel wave that had been hammered out of sheet steel.

Well, there I was all right. Philip Marlowe, intrepid sleuth, lisping tough-guy dialogue and making a play for an heiress with a husky voice and provocative manners. Sometimes I hate to look in the mirror, but this was as crazy as a wax museum. Nobody loves a private dick, especially the cops, but if this got around I wouldn't have to give them a fancy routine any more. They'd just laugh themselves to death.

It might be a gag, but I had to find out. One sure bet was that the character on screen was from back East. I could have wired New York for background, but there's nothing like doing your own legwork. Not when your leg gets pulled if you stand still.

It wasn't a hard one to crack, and what I dug up made me feel as happy as a starving flea on a fat dog. My *alter ego* was a West Side society doctor's son who'd become a juvenile lead on Broadway, then signed up with Warner Brothers when they were turning out gangster pictures where the guns fired blanks and a sock on the jaw was as real as a woman's promise. After a couple of sad martinis in a ritzy nightclub he liked to play tough, but no one ever had to hold him back hard enough to ruffle his bow tie.

I figured a way of stopping him. He'd been the Original Maude Humphrey Baby as a kid, simpering out of one of those baby-food ads. I picked up some copies and planned to show them around town. But then I heard he'd married the girl in the movie. Our penal code has a provision against double jeopardy, so why punish a loser twice?

It was weeping with rain when I landed in L.A., but I didn't want to think about rain, or tears, or anything moist except my fifth of bourbon.

BASIL RANSOME-DAVIES

SIR NOËL COWARD (1899–1973)

[*Scene: Two adjoining hotel balconies. Tropical evening. Moonlight. Somewhere a dance band is playing 'I'll see you again'.* ELYOT *and* AMANDA, *sophisticates in evening dress, come out on to their balconies.*]

ELYOT: Terribly chic, Noël.

AMANDA: Terribly, terribly chic. Did you know him well?

ELYOT: I worshipped him this side idolatory.

AMANDA: So did he, of course. Listen, they're playing his tune.

ELYOT: But not terribly well.

AMANDA: How too, too beastly of them!

ELYOT: He came from Teddington, you know.

AMANDA: How unutterably suburban of him. But it seemed to be the best thing to do if one is unfortunate enough to be born somewhere like that. To come from it at the earliest opportunity.

ELYOT: He went on the stage when he was very, very young. As a Lost Boy in *Peter Pan*.

AMANDA: And stayed with the fairies all his life.

ELYOT: What bitches you women are.

AMANDA: Did you ever see Noël by moonlight? I've always thought how attractive he would be by moonlight.

ELYOT: I always found him attractive. Especially in the twenties, with all those terribly clever plays: *The Vortex, Design for Living* . . . Do you remember, my darling?

AMANDA: It's the plays he did with Gertrude Lawrence that I remember best.

ELYOT: That is too, too understandable.

AMANDA: But *Private Lives* – Who can forget *Private Lives*? Or *Tonight at 8.30*?

ELYOT: And lunch at 'The Ivy' with Marie Tempest or Beatrice Lillie. It was all part of the pattern, my dear. All part of the rich, rich life of being a star. The footlights, the greasepaint and always the show had to go on. Always . . .

AMANDA: But he was terribly, terribly patriotic, Elyot.

ELYOT: Remember all those terribly, terribly patriotic plays and films – *Cavalcade, In Which We Serve* . . .

AMANDA: All that dying for Britain with brave little smiles on the lips.

ELYOT: Oh, he was utterly, utterly patriotic, was darling Noël.

AMANDA: Except when it came to paying his taxes. So in the end he had to live abroad.

ELYOT: How unutterably beastly of you, Amanda!

AMANDA: Isn't it true though?

ELYOT: Everyone knows that truth is far too unpleasant to be mentioned in polite society. Or even among one's friends.
  [*Enter* FRED.]

FRED: Here we are then, sir. Champagne for the toast. For the Master, as we all calls him.

AMANDA: How too, too perfect.

FRED: Only I hope you aren't going to be too long out of bed, on account of my feet. Killing me, they are. Besides you could do with the sleep, sir.

ELYOT: Who on earth goes to bed to sleep?

AMANDA: We shan't be long, Fred. I'll see to that.

FRED: I guessed you might, Miss. 'Sides, I've got this cracker of a housemaid waiting for me on the seventh floor.

AMANDA: Fred, your love life is a disgrace.

FRED: I know, Miss. Lovely, isn't it?
  [*Exit* FRED.]

ELYOT: I cannot imagine why I keep that man as my valet. He gets all the best laughs.

AMANDA: Never mind him, my darling. Fill the glasses. It's nearly midnight. Let's drink to the past of the Master whom we loved so dearly, and to his future too in this great British theatre of ours that he loved so much [*Her voice falters slightly*] . . . and let us hope that his dear darling comic plays will never ever become part of an examination syllabus.

ELYOT: I'll drink to that . . . Mandy.
  [*They drink. As the strains of 'Dance, dance, dance, Little Lady' swell, the curtain slowly falls.*]

E. O. PARROTT

'AL' CAPONE (1899–1947)

There are those who reckon that insisting on always being known
      as 'Capone' and never 'Capon*e*'
Was kind of phoney,
But Al saw himself as 100% American, like hamburgers or the
      Chrysler Building
And he wasn't above giving the lily a little gilding,
Such as claiming to be a native of New York City

When, like a lot of his fellow-banditti,
He wasn't so much Manhattan Metropolitan
As Neopolitan.
In any case he was mainly a big shot in Chicago, where the scope
    of his operations
Left a number of families severely short of relations,
And while most people can afford the loss of an odd nephew or
    cousin,
They tend to get sore when the missing list adds up to a dozen.
On the other hand, you could call him a guy with a mission
To make available to folks the kind of goods they weren't supposed
    to have under Prohibition
(Principally booze, but the fellow who likes booze is
More than likely also to be partial to such attractions as gambling
    and floozies).
As a go-ahead business tycoon, he figured competition was stupid,
And I guess it was if you were liable on St Valentine's Day to be
    visited by a gun-toting Cupid.
Al was a tough cookie all right; the only things that made him
    nervous
Were mentioning the scar on his cheek and agents of the Inland
    Revenue Service.
They finally sent him to the pen for failing to keep regular books,
And treating a prominent entrepreneur as though he were no better
    than out-and-out crooks
Would seem to indicate
That it's a hell of a taxing business to be head of the Syndicate.

BASIL RANSOME-DAVIES

ERNEST HEMINGWAY (1899–1961)

You know how it is when you read a Hemingway. There are the
words placed in order so that they make a definite statement, the
words short and simple, and all concrete. The words are simple,
with a simplicity that is deceptive. The sentences, too, are short.
Then there are the repetitions. With the shortness and simplicity
goes an effect of words being repeated.

Ernest Hemingway was a doctor's son from Chicago. I do
not say that in mockery, but only to be factual. Then, too, there

were the bullfights. But all that came later, with the marriages and the drink. In the war, which did not last very long for Ernest, there was drink and comradeship and the new feeling of being blown up. Being blown up by a trench-mortar missile was, in those days, a rare experience for Chicago boys. The Austrians designed their trench mortars so that they were able to kill and maim with great impartiality. If you were not killed there was a period of recuperation with nurses and, if you were lucky, wine. But the nurses did not last for ever and neither did the wine.

Afterwards for Ernest there was Paris and the writing. At first the writing was difficult and slow, with a difficulty and slowness that were the result of great discipline. Always, too, there was the need to think in a disciplined way, and with great care, so that what you wrote would be true, stated truly and in a disciplined way, therefore it would be truthful and of a great newness. But this too did not last.

For Ernest knowing the real thing, without tricks or faking, and to be sure that the reader, reading it, would see that it was real and not a deception, was important. Knowing it and rendering it truly, all the words fitted together with an honest passion, knowing and feeling as surely as you feel the tug of a marlin on your line out in the gulf, truthfully, passionately, all coming together and going away, the earth moving, and without deception. If a writer truly practised this his work would live.

I do not think it fair to blame the drink and the marriages and the bullfights. A man may have all these and survive. But America does not want its writers to survive. If an American writer writes the truth he will become rich and famous, and the riches and the fame will make him blind and he will no longer see the truth, or want to write it. But Ernest was some guy.

BASIL RANSOME-DAVIES

ERIC BLAIR ('GEORGE ORWELL') (1903–50)

The Ladybird George Orwell

This is Eric. Eric's mummy and daddy have some money. They send him to a good school. 'Bye 'bye, Eric!

It is a bad school. Eric is not happy. He goes to a better school, but he is still not happy.

Eric goes to help look after a far-away land. There are brown-skinned people in that land. Eric does not like the way the brown-skinned people are looked after. It's not fair, he says. He goes home.

Eric has no money. He washes dishes and makes friends with other people who have no money. He writes about them in a book. People buy Eric's book.

Eric says: 'I no longer want to be Eric. I shall be George from now on. George writes books! Please call me George.'

George goes to another foreign land. Some good men are fighting with some bad men. George wants to help the good men. He helps them, but some of the good men become bad men. Some of the bad men who were good men say that George's friends are really bad men. George is cross with them. He writes a book. The bad men win.

George hears about another land where there are bad men pretending to be good men. He feels cross. He writes a book. In the book the bad men are pigs. In the end the bad pigs become bad men.

George is ill. He goes to a far-away island. He thinks the world is full of bad men. The bad men always beat the good men in the end. He writes a sad book. The book is about the last good man in the world. The good man cannot beat all the bad men. The bad men always win.

George dies. 'Bye 'bye, George!

PETER NORMAN

LEON BISMARCK ('BIX') BEIDERBECKE (1903–31)

Born of solid, bourgeois German stock,
Long before such beastly things as Rock,
Leon Bismarck, better known as 'Bix',
Grew up in Iowa, out in the sticks.

Self-taught, he was an infant prodigy,
And played piano from the age of three,
But after learning cornet at fourteen,
He quickly made his name upon the scene,
For Bix's bell-like tone and matchless style
Stood out from other players by a mile.

He worked the Great Lakes steamers in his teens,
And later joined the famous Wolverines,
And then Paul Whiteman, self-styled 'King of Jazz',
Whose style was more like jumped-up razzmatazz.

Bix wrote for piano – here's a shortish list:
'Flashes', 'Candlelights' and 'In a Mist';
He had a taste for atmospheric titles,
And harmonies which activate the vitals;
He'd learned a trick or two from Debussy
And Eastwood Lane (whoever he may be).

He practised cornet mostly, sometimes piano,
But not *mens sana in corpore sano*,
And boozed his way through so-called Prohibition,
Maintaining thus a good old jazz tradition.

So Bismarck slowly sank towards his fate:
(He hopped the twig at only twenty-eight),
And though his every note on wax is prized,
His real potential went unrealized;
Just think of what he might have done, by gosh,
If only he had stuck to orange squash!

RON RUBIN

WILLIAM JOYCE (1906–46)

His father was Irish, his mother a Brit,
Although William was born a New Yorker;
But the quirks of his birth didn't bother a bit
All the judges that sentenced this talker.

From Brooklyn to Mayo in Ireland he came
As a kid, long before later folly;
At fifteen in London, his first claim to fame
Was a course at the Battersea Poly.

Later on, at the Univ. of London enrolled,
For their Officer Corps he applied,
For 'the country which I love so dearly', whose fold
He passed into with passionate pride.

187

As a Fascist, he clashed as a student. His face
Was indelibly scarred by a razor.
Was his thought, as he fought, of a pure British place,
And what happens to one that betrays her?

A philologist, even psychologist, Will
Was a learned post-graduate, eager.
A Tory, a Mosleyite; further right still –
His own National Socialist Leaguer.

His League had a shop selling truncheons and knives;
He was twice let off, charged with assault;
And then, before war, his big moment arrives,
When he left (with his passport at fault)

For Hamburg. In weeks, he was minding a mike,
And burbled for Goebbels with pleasure;
He spoke of the folk that the Glorious Reich
Had provided with more than their measure.

The tosh that he talked sounded painfully posh,
Like a monocled donkey, or mynah,
And his 'Germany calling' disrupted the nosh
Of the British (who thought him a whiner).

'Lord Haw-Haw' was born and the music-halls rang
As his Michael was duly extracted;
His jaw-jaw was poor; but it meant that he'd hang
When the law wanted vengeance exacted.

Till the end of the war, his aforementioned voice
Could be heard heiling Hitler was best;
They caught 'Wilhelm Hansen' – yes, William Joyce –
He was shot in the leg on arrest.

His passports to fate meant a wait. Was it proper
To hang him? For where was he born?
In Brooklyn. But Justice, for nothing could stop her,
Had him hanged not too long after dawn.

The crowd called aloud with a mixture of mirth
And elation when notice was posted;
But why fear a fool, irrespective of birth?
Was it merely the fact that he *boasted*?

BILL GREENWELL

188

SIR JOHN BETJEMAN (1906–84)

Sir John Betjeman, Sir John Betjeman,
Rhyming and chiming as only you can,
It seemed like a love-match – but didn't last long,
(I frequently ask myself where we went wrong).

You told me that night as we sat in the car,
Of your Marlborough schooldays – you still bore the scar,
And your time up at Oxford, enjoying the search,
As you walked down the High, for the highest High Church.

A poet from boyhood, no shadow of doubt,
You spoke of the things you were writing about,
From stockbroker Surrey to plainsong, and how
You hated the bulldozer, concrete, and Slough.

Years later, on T.V., you opened our eyes
To the beauty of buildings we'd come to despise,
And tirelessly fought to secure the survival
Of Victoriana and Gothic Revival.

By now you were famous, one of the *élite*
Of poets beloved by the man in the street,
And heading the short list when Day-Lewis passed,
Fittingly, you were made Laureate at last.

All through your life you were mindful of Death,
And you met him at last on the way to Polzeath,
In that far Cornish haven where He set you free,
Summoned by bells ringing over the sea.

STANLEY J. SHARPLESS

I was born a true Edwardian before the war for Serbia,
With a penchant for the parish-church and passion for suburbia.
I was an antiquarian, a critic for the *Telegraph*,
With a jolly sort of twinkle and a surreptitious belly-laugh.

At Marlborough and Oxford I was not so keen on studying,
As hooting at the brutalists whose noses needed bloodying;
I haunted railway stations whose destruction I was sorry at,
And the public purse repaid my verse by making me the Laureate.

189

In praise of *Coronation Street*, few pensioners were scattier,
While the local belfries never knew a warden any battier;
The knighthood for my writing, which was technically professional,
Suggests the Queen admired scenes with which I was obsessional.

My theme was Surrey virgins on their horses, hardly bulkier,
Although the county planners made my verse a little sulkier;
And God assisted me in death – a subtle, slightly early fate,
To cheer up my chum Philip, as he glumly neared the pearly gate.

BILL GREENWELL

W. H. AUDEN (1907–73)

Yesterday all the past: the mother's womb opening
At a medical father's probing; the prep-school,
    The study of geology and sodomy at Oxford,
Yesterday the third-class degree and the obscure teaching.

Yesterday the dominance of left-wing literary journals,
The tours of German boys and China with Isherwood,
    Yesterday the plays, half-verse, half-prose. The
Youthful notoriety, the abortive trip to Spain.

Yesterday the final remaining in America,
The blonde lover-collaborator and the lecture circuit;
    Yesterday the abuse of deserter,
From warring England; but today the poems.

Tomorrow the lonely old man endlessly repeating
His set pieces at High Table, the fruitless attempt
    At a haven in Oxford; the legend
Of peeing in the sink and vast amounts of drinking,

The virtuoso technician and the face like a wedding cake
Left out in the rain; the librettist for Stravinsky,
    The religious routines, the translations
Of Bertolt Brecht, but today the poems.

REM BEL

IAN LANCASTER FLEMING (1908–64)

'Knew his father,' mused Sir Walter. 'Valentine Fleming. Tory M.P. for South Oxfordshire. Appropriate – after all, he owned most of it. Went west at Arras in '17. Left four topping lads. Peter the eldest, then Ian.'

Young Sandy steeled himself for yet another display of old Bullivant's all-too-total recall. At 101, he was – though an obvious dotard – still the most dynamic Head the Secret Service had ever known. Time and again, when one of his innumerable predecessors had defected, he had been hauled back into temporary harness. At least, the government had conceded that, as it was patently impossible to find a single other member of the Service who was not either alcoholic, paederastic, or clandestinely a full Colonel in the K.G.B. – usually all three – it was simpler to give him a lifetime lien on the job.

'A shade overshadowed at Eton by Peter,' Bullivant bumbled on, 'but he was *Victor Ludorum* two years on the trot – a feather in any feller's cap. Sandhurst for a spell – then wanderlust got him as it gets any man with any spunk in 'im. But,' he chuckled, 'I don't need to tell an Arbuthnot *that*.'

'Indeed no, sir.' Young Sandy smiled back. 'But what you ought to know is . . .'

But Sir Walter was far too snugly settled in the saddle of senile reminiscence to listen. 'Didn't make it into the F O – bad show – scribbled for Reuter's – banked and stockbroked for a bit – a Commander in Naval Intelligence in the second big shindig – then a gossip wallah on one of the Sundays. Married Anne – one of the Charteris gels – already been spliced to Rothermere, the yellow press peddler. Then he started spinning these spiffing yarns of his. Can't say that I cared for that James Bond chappie. Bit of an outsider – not quite the white man – rank bad form in my book. However . . . Pity Ian burnt himself out so young. Too fond of the ladies – bless 'em – looked too long on the wine when it was red – all that sort of thing. Of course, you, young Sandy, were too young ever to have met him.'

'On the contrary, sir, I saw him only last week.'

Bullivant sat stupefied as he went quickly on. 'For reasons I needn't go into, I was following the caravan trail to Bumsuk disguised as a Kurd eunuch – as you know, I'm one of the few living Englishmen with perfect Outer Mongolian – one never knows when one's going to need these little-yellow-men's lingoes.

We passed a caravan going the other way to Longkok – and there was something in the cut of the jib of one of the camel drivers – I knew at once. Believe me, sir, Ian's not *dead* – men like Ian don't just die! He's out there still – in the field – playing the Great Game – the Greatest Game there is – and, what's more, he's still playing it on Our Side!'

Sir Walter's eyes shone with a truly apocalyptic light. 'The Great Game,' he wheezed, 'Our Side, the True Breed, the Endless Story – England!' Unlike the perfect vodka martini, he was deeply stirred but totally unshaken.

MARTIN FAGG

DYLAN THOMAS (1914–53)

Look. He is born now, sobbing seagull-squab fury, shaking red fists, red, unread, shivertimbering the cradle with new rage at the cat-calling world.

It's me, Caitlin. Smiling gypsy-eyebrowed from Bohemia, who's my little wonder.

Blind Captain Thomas, every day a blinder, stands on his step to say his poetry. Oh, my deaf darlings, nothing in your pockets but cut-glass visiting cards. Where are the cosy fivers, cheques to warm the bottom of my glass?

Bowery flowery West Side girls, fishnet flashing in split silky skirts, oh, Dylan bach, how could you? Easy, says Captain Thomas.

He is gone now, gone from the skittle-alleying sawdust, gone from beer as flat as a sermon. Listen. The red fists still shake.

ALISON PRINCE

It's Not As If

It's not as if the quarter-miling hares
Lammed by the mooing wind above the barns
Gave the bright boy of Wales a special licence
    To snare our struggling language.

It's not as if the slightest care for syntax
Troubled the meaning of this poet mister;
Make me some phrases from the windbag pictures
    Will spell you out his sayings.

It's not as if the transatlantic ravers
Let him go gentle into fuddled darkness
Or turned the broken syllables to sunshine
    Before his fatal midnight.

It's not as if, his umpteenth year to heaven
Closing on Dylan in the dumbfound daisies,
His absence hymned by snivelling boys in jerseys
    Can do for him twice over.

It's not as if his sermoned faults, whose echoes
Ring from the synagogues of Sunday papers,
Alter the wit and wonder of his giving
    Colour to human chaos.

PAUL GRIFFIN

ORSON WELLES (1915–85)

A whizz-kid from the start, brass-necked and manic,
His notoriety boomed with his weight.
Those Wellesian-Wellsian Martians were a panic
Like Hitler back in 1938.

At R.K.O. he had a boy's own dream:
Carte blanche, 'the biggest train-set in the world'.
He Kaned a pompous magnate's self-esteem,
And burned his boats where 'Rosebud' cracked and curled.

Rambunctious scholar-gypsy ever after,
He earned his bread from vivid cameos,
Never without a glint of wicked laughter
Under the wig, moustache or putty nose.

The joke is endless, like the mirror-maze
In *Lady from Shanghai*. Is Orson Welles
Created by the characters he plays
Or are they just his double-bluffing shells?

Perhaps 'Franz Kafka' is a pseudonym,
'Shakespeare' another cunning *nom-de-guerre*,
And Welles is both of them. Or are they *him*?
Who knows? We seek him here, we seek him there . . .

When death sought him he puffed on his cigar
And wheezed and chuckled going where death beckoned,
Musing the paradox of cinema
That 'Film is truth twenty-four times a second.'

BASIL RANSOME-DAVIES

ROBERT LOWELL (1917–77)

Being a Boston Lowell is a fate
That shakes a cocktail of desire and hate
For old New England. Puritans would raid
The red man's hearth and nursery. Then they prayed.
When Robert prayed, God told him to resist
The war compulsion. Punks who won't enlist
Are hushed off to the jailhouse. In his cell
He felt his poetry stir up like hell
And poured it out in thick, tormented lines.
Rome's remedies all blooped. When faith declines
What can a man do but get wired on speed
And frantic slugs of liquor? Out of need
He sold the true confessions of his life:
How he went bananas and beat his wife.
His verse snarled like a wounded dog within
Lord Weary's Castle. Sin-scales on his skin,
He glittered, grew to love celebrity.
But wouldn't dance at Johnson's jamboree.
Outpointing Mailer as the peaceniks' choice,
He slammed the war in a sore, crusty voice.
Yet everything breaks. A stretched heart can slump
During a cab ride like a worn-out pump.

BASIL RANSOME-DAVIES

PHILIP LARKIN (1922–85)

Philip Larkin Sends a Postcard Home

Here I am, shelved at last.
Even thinking about it used to leave me aghast,
Now I realize there's a lot to be said
For being dead.

I miss Hull,
Where life was splendidly dull,
And I miss the feeling of being deprived,
On which I thrived.

As University Librarian
I was accused by one man of being a vulgarian
For writing: 'Books are a load of crap.'
(I replied: 'Pure masochism, old chap.')

I wonder who
Thought up the Larkin Westminster Abbey Memorial do,
With all that episcopal razzamatazz?
Nice of them to include some jazz.

'The best Laureate we never had.'
As epitaphs go, that's not bad;
A safe verdict, now I'm out of sight,
I almost think it's almost right.

STANLEY J. SHARPLESS

Once he was sure the midwife nodded off,
He nipped out quick, for crafty sips of milk.
At least, that's how you'd fancy it: a scoff
For starters. Scribblers of the Larkin ilk,
Shy, unassertive, fear a real immersion
In life, although you'd think him kid enough
To hop the cemetery wall, and sprawled
In long grass, thumb his nose at Saul's conversion.
Was he bespectacled already? Bald?

The prompter in the wings, by this first stage
He must have twigged his folks, running to form,
Would screw him up like paper. *Turn the page*;
Bike idly; *switch the wireless up*. His norm
Might once have muddled Coventry, in the collar

Ringing the neck of wood, the suburb's edge
From which he jumped. His records, rather jazzy,
Belied his look, a blinking Oxford scholar.
He liked their subtle blues, and shunned the snazzy.

And there was something clerical, if odd,
That muted talent, blurred the lambent eyes
Above his parson's nose. His brush with God
Was more a brush-off; one of those curt replies
One hears, half-hurtful, when the dicky heart
Just isn't in it. Strolling round a quad,
With Amis or with Wain, he hunted fiction,
Finding it in a church, if not in art.
His verse became more proper jurisdiction.

Novels, yes; but in a world of books,
A shadow moving strangely through the shades
Of intellect, through stories banked in stacks,
He turned away. And fatuous parades,
That damn romantic pose of Dylan Thomas
Waving a whisky, sent him into nooks
And crannies where one blends, as merely local.
He set about restoring sense, and commas,
Or writing words whose meanings were bifocal.

A library with pages licked and lifted,
In Belfast, and in Leicester – then to Hull,
From which he rarely wanted to be shifted,
Even at Whitsuntide. What's tedious, or dull
To other artists, this he found congenial.
His act was solo. Many lines were sifted,
Composed, arranged, removed, deleted, picked,
And poetry for him was almost menial,
A process by which bricks were bricked, unbricked.

At last, he nabbed a literary slumber,
Choosing his moment, keeping margins straight.
His daily chores, a stroll along the Humber
Were quite sufficient, dwelling on the fate
He knew did not await him, though the cheers
Of critics, in a most peculiar number,
Must have amused him. Writing was *required*,
To pay the rent of fame, still in arrears;
He ducked his head, and shied from being hired.

A serious bloke, mock-serious by turns,
In whose effacing person readers sought
A hint of something fiery, as burns
In those who like their poems to be taught.
Instead, he liked to brandish his rosette,
Blue as forget-me-not, spurning the concerns
With which his fans invested him. The press
Might simply snap his stub of cigarette;
What spent his life was ordering his stress.

BILL GREENWELL

MARIA CALLAS (1923–77)

Synopsis of *Maria*, an Opera in Four Acts

ACT I

A village in Epirus: 1943. Partisans kill German prisoners by way
of limbering up to kill one another. *Parsifal*, seventeen-year-old
Colonel in Waffen SS, sings of unspotted maiden he will never
now wed ('My Lily of the Lamp-Light'). Enter *Maria*, mule-
trekking through mountains in university vac. *Xanthippe*, local
matriarch (has buried most relatives) hails her as future *Prima
Donna* bestriding world stage ('I've just met a girl called Maria').
In impassioned *scena*, *Maria* points to peaks above, from which
numberless matrons have flung themselves rather than be ravished
by invader. All village women rush off to do likewise, while men
enjoy coffee, brandy and *baclava* and sing of bonds of fraternity
binding all Greeks. Flame-throwing Tiger tanks, cataclysmic
earthquake and Titanic thunderstorm simultaneously assault village
as *Maria* rides serenely on.

ACT II

An Athens courtyard: 1945. *Maria's Mother* bemoans her
daughter's gross obesity. Enter *Spirit of Sigmund Freud*. He
diagnoses *Maria's* nineteen-stone *enbonpoint* as hysterical symptom
correctable by expert vocal training. Three hundred fellow students
join *Maria* in Attic Giggling Song. End of German War
announced. Run of Greek Civil War to continue indefinitely.
Various notabilities drop in. In sublime Sextet, *Archbishop
Damaskinos*, *Churchill*, *Roosevelt*, *Stalin*, *Vera Lynn* and *Maria*
sing of age-old folly of Man and pleasures of Peace.

ACT III

Scene I: *Maria's* dressing-room at *La Scala*. She now thin as lath.
Enter decrepit husband *Meneghini*, bearing dozen red roses. He
falls under weight. Tenderly she lifts and thanks him ('Oh my
beloved Sugar-Daddy'). He responds with sparkling Patter Song
('Ouzo lucky boy then'). Attendants revive him with oxygen as
Maria laments indignity of marriage to impotent dotard daily
lavishing billions of lire on her. She departs for First Act entrance
in *Tosca*. As sound of ovation greeting her is heard, her dresser
Xanthippe, now 103, drops dead, singing meanwhile of her adored
Maria ('We'll meet again').

Scene II: *Maxim's* in Paris: later that evening. *Maria* the universal
toast. *Ari Onassis* orders bubbly by the jeroboam and, in tenor
cantilena, boasts of being wealthiest man in world ('I may look
fairly filthee, but I'm filthee filthee rich'). This becomes duet as
Maria confesses to instant attraction he has for her. During
frenzied supper-scene – out Travving 'Traviata' – he whispers
sweet somethings in her ear.

ACT IV

Maria's Paris apartment. Her *Bonne* sings of her mistress's
disappointments. *Ari* never proposed. *Maria's* voice lies in ruins.
Comeback Recital Tour has proved bathetic farce. *Maria* enters,
aged beyond belief. In 'These I have lived for', she looks back over
career; and, in 'Oh fatal gift', bewails that global *réclame* has
brought scant happiness. She bitterly derides scheming widow
supplanting her in *Ari's* affections ('Yakkety-Yakkety Yucky
Yacky'). A telex arrives: *Ari* has married *Jackie*. After wrecking
apartment, *Maria* sinks, dying – 'Don't weep for me, *La Scala*!'
Curtain.

MARTIN FAGG

ELVIS PRESLEY (1935–77)

Spasmodic ghost of an imaginary twin, the boy came out of a land,
Mississippi, mute, but never quiescent in its long, unforgiving
recuperation from a nemetic justice more venomous, pride-swollen,
iron-bound than the evils it was sworn to harrow from the cotton-
eroded earth. Its inhabitants, no longer garlanded with the bright
plumes of Lee's army, morose and impotent with the furious and

198

suspended rage of a banished suitor, drew their wisdom from ancient whispered stories of blood and faith.

While Vernon dreamed his quick-money dreams behind the locked gates of Parchman, the boy huddled in the soft female drench of the sheets with Gladys, the awesome, never-to-be-forgotten mother. If out of her lullabies he was drawn to sketch the lineaments of his own fate in song, it must have been with a tremulous abatement of all credulity that he heard the verdict *Boy, you sound jest like a nigrah*. And then: *Boy, you're surely white*.

It was the Colonel (in harsh jest, or proleptic of future triumphant campaigns?) who amplified that muttered observation of destiny into a dionysiac frenzy poured from drug-store juke boxes, animating to writhing tumescence the limbs and bodies of shuffling youths, then tuned it to a mellow, patriotic fanfare delivered from atop a blubber-mountain of silk, paste and raw gold in the dead air of gambling palaces.

And the boy lived in photographs, now shorn, in khaki, peering like a shy and apprehensive gopher from the turret of a tank, now with Priscilla, herself androgynously cosmetized like the very incarnation of the lost twin, ritualistically conjoined like the interlocking pieces of a plastic puzzle. Or at Gracelands, the mansion built out of, stuffed with, gewgaws and gadgets as if out of a necrotic passion to waste the saturating riches of his own guilty survival, the king in a domain of efflorescent and specious grandeur.

Finally, puffed and elephantine with a fierce (though ardent and – yes – unregretted) surfeit of blackened and downhome bacon ('Jest like Maw used to cook'), burgers, sodas and shakes – adding, for just measure, an insane pharmacopoeia of sense-obliterating drugs – the aging half-orphan could only drool, as thickly and automatically as pump-engine, his slow, involuntary epitaph: *Don't Be Cruel*.

BASIL RANSOME-DAVIES

NOTES ON THE CONTRIBUTORS

(In which they do not spare themselves)

O. BANFIELD (b. 1915)

Born under Leo, during World War One,
I half remember all the flags and fun.
At Armistice, when I was only three,
And fell downstairs, drunk with hilarity;
It raised a bump like Juliet's on my brow,
And left a fear of heights which lasts till now.

Things always were a shade mistimed for me –
Though Swansea-bred, I ne'er met Dylan T.
I studied German, but War Two broke out;
I read, not speak it – Hitler's fault, no doubt.
Bad at exams, I got a Double Second,
So I was doomed. The Civil Service beckoned,

First to Llandudno, fair and peaceful spot,
Then off to London, where the war was hot.
There, in Intelligence, behind the scenes –
You'd love to know – *I* dare not spill the beans.
'And now, I'll be a journalist,' I said,
But couldn't, so I married one instead.

I wanted kids, though it was late to start,
Each good at singing, poetry or art.
Our union after three long years was blessed
With one small girl, a triple-vintage pest,
By neighbours hated and by school abhorred,
And all the little boys for miles adored.

I'd longed to be a poet all my days,
But it's my daughter who goes in for lays.
Though some reviewers think she is a bitch,
Her *Sky Ray Lolly*'s making Chatto rich.
My life's been dull, but still I've done my bit
To aid the sacred cause of English lit.

REM BEL (b. 1956)

FROM 'NEW MUSIC EXPRESS'

So I'm walking along this once grandiose, now down-at-heel street in dour
old Edinburgh. I stop at a row of names. Rem's bed-sit is a tip, but at
least it's on the ground-floor. Rem has a well-built yet slim yet strong

cyclist's body and a ten-speeder leaning against a crammed bookcase. Behind the National Health gold frames, cowpat coloured eyes gleam. 'That's very appropriate – my father was a dairy farmer in New Zealand.' And the hair, the colour of red brick? 'Same as the university I went to, Victoria, in Wellington, New Zealand.' Less the ivy? Rem smirks.

Learn anything there? 'Eng. Lit. and Latin. That got me a scholarship to Edinburgh University, but I chucked it in to sell post-cards at Edinburgh Castle, to be a civil servant and to write.' What about being published? 'Hardly at all. Will write anything. Have you got a buyer for a libretto for a light opera on nuclear power or a situation comedy about a community programme?' Are those going damp in the desk then? 'Haven't got a desk. And I haven't written them yet. But just name the price.'

What about the dosh then? 'I teach people how to process words on machines. Not to produce them, just process them.' A sigh. A clip at one heavy white toe-nail with a pair of orange handled scissors . . . (And so on for three more columns.)

GERARD BENSON (b. 1931)

Yes, and to get to the biographical details, as I was bound to, sooner or later. I was born, I shall try to treat the matter calmly, no worse an experience than many a later event in my life (you'd swear it *was* mine) in Golders Green in 1931, of parents impeccably Irish and with a sister (that is, a nun) in attendance, but to pass on . . . attempts were made to educate me (*quo lux ducit*), not least at Rendcomb or perhaps Rendcombe College in the Gloucestershire hill country. Ups and downs. Ups and downs. And the year of chagrin. To continue this inexhaustible narrative, I entered the Royal Navy, its most lubberly sailor, then the theatrical profession, then that of teaching and became a lecturer, a man paid to talk by the hour, at the Central School of Speech and Drama, having on my meandering path collected marriages and children . . . but all this is to ignore the years, the aeons it seems, yes, it seems aeons, of stardom as Barrow Poet (not to mention Gerard and Jean) trundling my cart of music (oh yes) and of poetry through the known world (if it can be said to be known) and singing, speaking and clowning – I remember clowning, I am certain of it. But I tire of this mode and would talk again of true love. I married Catherine . . . and lived happily ever after. Isn't that what they say?

W. S. BROWNLIE

In a funk in a tank, in the war,
He would often wonder: 'What for?'
      Yet he joined the T.A.,
      No, not for the pay;
It was more for the *esprit de corps*.

There was training and things of that sort;
Also dining, and passing the port.
    What with parties nocturnal,
    And being a Colonel,
He rated it rather good sport.

He taught thirty-three years in a school,
And enjoyed it a lot, as a rule,
    But as standards went down,
    He said with a frown:
'That's your lot. I'm for out. I'm no fool.'

Now retired, this contented old Scot
Has developed a bit of a pot.
    And when offered a drink,
    Without pausing to think,
He says 'whisky' more often than not.

V. ERNEST COX

If I'd been born in Hampstead instead of Wolverhampton,
    If I'd been upper-class not Jack-the-lad,
If my tendency to truant from school had been stamped on,
    If I'd have been an Oxford undergrad.

If instead of youth work training I'd decided to read law,
    If I'd written all the books inside my head,
If acute procrastination wasn't my most telling flaw,
    If two years ago at forty I'd dropped dead.

If I'd preferred Beethoven to the Beatles – 'Yeah, yeah, yeah',
    If I hadn't followed Wolves home and away,
If instead of getting married I'd lived life solitaire,
    If I hadn't got two sons to turn me grey.

If I didn't live in Hertfordshire – in Welwyn Garden City,
    If I didn't earn my crust at County Hall,
If all that's happened to me hadn't happened – what a pity,
    For then I wouldn't be the chap I am at all.

MARTIN FAGG

Always almost getting somewhere, he rarely, if ever, *got*:
His life was one long side-track, he browsed and mooched a lot.
A dilettante butterfly,
Seduced by whims that flutter by,

He'd be tracing, say, some gilded words of the precious Walter Pater,
And still be riffling through the dictionary of quotations five hours later,
Without ever having found the original *mot*
Though.
Killed with his pet seal when five tons of paper fell through the ceiling
    and pinned 'em –
Well, what can you expect if you let books multiply like something out of
    a novel by John Wyndham?
His mind was wry, ironic, styptic, sceptic, brittle:
He knew about a lot of things – but only a very little.

BILL GREENWELL

Bill Greenwell was Caesarean,
    September '52,
In Sunderland, of Georgian egg
    (Conceivably, that's true);

His baby-face, then hairless, was
    A Coronation mug.
He grew, and so on. Then there bit
    The Competition Bug.

He's drifted down to Exeter,
    A teacher. There he lingers.
Define him – an obsessive sort;
    But type him – he's two fingers.

PAUL GRIFFIN (b. 1922)

PAUL GRIFFIN was a perfect curse
At talking to his nurse in verse.
His Army and his Cambridge times
Were constantly disgraced by rhymes.
What chance was there for such a creature
Other than as an English teacher?
And when his colleagues were all dead
Of boredom, he became a Head.
After long years inflicting pain
On children, he hung up his cane.
'Enough of sticks; I need a carrot!'
He cried; and wrote for Eric Parrott.

MARY HOLTBY

In Oxford's fair city, where dons are so witty,
    I first oped my eyes on this valley of tears;
Though Oxford's my *heimat*, so vile is the climate
    It forced me to board for my formative years.
Advancement of learning secured my returning,
    To sit at a number of eminent feet.
'Not to toil as a teacher nor partner a preacher' –
    I broke both these vows when my course was complete.
Through Kent, Yorkshire, Singapore, Malvern, Fate's finger
    Propelled me to Oxford again for a while;
I studied the sources of Dean Donne's discourses
    Until (with three children) we moved to Carlisle.
My mate turned commuter; itinerant tutor
    (Committed to 'comping'), to Purley I went;
Then lastly in Chichester Destiny pitches
    (Who knows for how long now?) my travel-stained tent.

TIM HOPKINS

EPITAPH ON A TEACHER

Taught metre and rhyme,
To brats and worse,
To buy the time,
To write this verse.

JOYCE JOHNSON

She feels her life cannot be interesting
To anyone who reads this book for fun.
It offers very little scope for jesting.
This task is not at all an easy one.

She's earned her bread by illustrating Blyton
Assisted by the crosswords she has done.
So long as she has stuff to draw or write on,
She finds her lot to be a happy one.

Among her many founts of delectation
The countryside affords a major part.
Her epitaph could well be the quotation:
'Nature she loved, and, next to Nature, Art.'

To changing scenes of life she has adjusted,
Had lucky and some not-so-lucky spells,
But never yet has signed herself 'Disgusted',
Although she now resides in Tunbridge Wells.

ARDA LACEY

'Arda long time no have see. She likee plentee
go-go-go. Stop Shanghai, Singapore, Africa,
New Zealand, Australia. Catchee two man, two
children, four-piece gland-daughters.'
     'Letter say "all man likee Chinese chow,
swim, tennis, tlavel. No time glow old. Plentee
busy litee. B'long seclet sclibe society London.
Now stop long-time England Kent. No more hoppity-hop." '

RUSSELL LUCAS

Russell Lucas, born,
east of Suez, Capricorn,
somewhere in Bombay.
     Lancs, Cumbria, Kent,
     early life was quite ill-spent,
     all work, little play.
Soldier, salesman, clerk,
just an ordinary jerk,
then in Beds, was wed.
     Labour Party, sprogs,
     anti-Tory but pro dogs,
     reasonably read.
Nabokov, Proust, Joyce,
Barthes, Borges, are his choice,
and Waugh, who's lighter.
Banking and F.X.,
life was slightly more complex,
now, just a writer.

T. L. McCARTHY

Born at the turn of the century to a noble Glasgow-Irish family, he was
educated at Daisy Street Mixed Infants, Eton and Oxford. After he had
been sent down, a great future was predicted for him in the world of
letters and his encyclopaedic and impeccably researched *Bouzouki
Tavernas of Greece* won high critical acclaim and is still accepted as the

definitive work on the subject. A liking for fast women, slow horses and 'Auld Kirkyaird' Scotch whisky ('The Late Laird's Choice') led, however, to his downfall. The family estates were sequestrated, his friends deserted him and he now ekes out a frugal living writing doggerel from a mean suite of rooms overlooking London's Hyde Park.

PHILIP A. NICHOLSON (b. 1924)

Born in Oldham – '24,
Left school early, went to war,
Flew in Lancs, earned daily bread
As teacher, left with rank of Head,
Obsessive love affair with rhyme
Doodles madly all the time –
Doesn't smoke and seldom drinks,
Gone to earth in Fenland Lincs.

PETER NORMAN

In a Lancashire town known as Oldham,
Not noted for fresh air or fun,
Mr and Mrs A. Norman
Had a daughter and then had a son.

But then – ah! removal so dear to me, dear to me! –
They settled in Dorset; 'tis clear to me, clear to me,
That these lines, penned whilst crossing a bridge o'er the Piddle,
Owe their birth to my spring-time's long, Hardyesque idyll.

I have seen the best minds of my generation getting pissed on Tartan
    Bitter in provincial universities,
Hammering English as a foreign language into thick Norwegians,
Sharing flats with psychedelic walls in Shepherd's Bush,
Looning about and wilfully damaging their hearing to the Star Spangled
    Hendrix Stratocaster feedback experience.

Peter, Peter,
quiet commuter,
now you've got a
home computer.

PHYLLIS PARKER

'Cheshire born and Cheshire bred
Strong i'th arm and wick i'th yead'

Not quite true, but from Cow Lane, Norley, via Newnham I got as far as Brazil (courtesy of Vestey's) and then back to London and all kinds of jobs. Kept writing and enjoyed it – had enough success to keep going – anyway you can't help it, can you? One great bonus is that friends made through writing are such good friends.

E. O. PARROTT

[*The sounds of glasses clinking mingle with rural rhubarb. We are in 'The Bull', Ambridge.*]

SID PERKS: Parrott? E. O. Parrott? Isn't he that writer chap? Lives on that old Dutch barge on the Regent's Canal?

WALTER: That's him, me old beauty. Did that Penguin Limerick book with all them saucy verses . . . He-he-he!

CLARRIE: I don't think I want to hear them, Mr Gabriel.

SID P: There is also them literary books, you know . . . *How to Become Ridiculously Well-Read in One Evening.*

CLARRIE: What I don't see is why a degree in Geography, when he's so keen on poetry and that?

NELSON: One can also have other interests.

SID: Cockney feller, he is. Born within sound of Bow Bells.

NELSON: How noisy for him. But he was brought up in Sussex.

WALTER: But he did his war service near here. Working at that radar place before becoming a cart . . . a cartoggygrapher. Though why he should start drawing carts . . .

CLARRIE: That's map drawing, Mr Gabriel. Even I knows about Admirality charts . . .

NELSON: And all the time writing and doing amateur dramatics . . .

SID: He was a teacher too at Havering for fourteen years.

NELSON: Where, I am sure, it seemed twice the time.

CLARRIE: Then he had to retire, 'cos his eyes were bad. Poor chap . . .

NELSON: Still, he has published all these books. Five, isn't it? But why did he take us on to do his biography?

CLARRIE: He liked the idea of having it in a pub. Got a soft spot for pubs, he has.

NOEL PETTY

Noel Petty was born up on t'moors
(Though the actual event was indoors)
Which accounts for his daze
And his rough Northern ways
And occasional Heathcliff-like roars.

The Queen's shilling was his first fee
(It turned out to be 20p).
After that, by the Cam,
He managed to sham
Enough maths to acquire a degree.

Computery then was the trend,
And the States was his next journey's end,
But now his vocation
Is vaticination
(Go on, look it up, don't pretend).

He affects an antiqueness of style,
Has whiskers all over his dial,
Writes pantos and romps,
And wins a few comps,
Sings alto, and bows a mean viol.

FIONA PITT-KETHLEY (b. 1954)

'Look what the stork's brought in!' my mother said,
In 1954. (She was in bed.)
I was the busiest of little sods,
Built altars round the house to Pagan Gods,
Stuck pennies in the locks in ones or twos,
(I thought all doors were slot-machines or loos),
I peed in model village castle moats
And looked up ladies' skirts or tweaked their coats.
The best years of my life were not the best –
I hated school and hated it with zest.
I drew the teachers, pulled legs off their chairs,
Made rhymes about their greying pubic hairs.
My Art School was much better, much more free.
We used to drink a lot and not just tea.
I ushered at the Old Vic in the nights,
Saw all the plays for free and other sights.
My friends were all more than a little camp.
We went through every style from tramp to vamp.
I dyed my hair each shade from blonde to black
And once went flashing in a dirty mac.
I left with a B.A. Hons. in Fine Art,
Which proved no way to an employer's heart.
I've searched for work, both near and far from home –
I even tried a monastery in Rome.
I've taught English to kids, Art to the old,
And shivered as an extra in the cold –

And all to subsidize my *full-time* verse.
(A lack of money's always been my curse.)
My home's on the South Coast, and some would say,
It's like a brothel that has had its day.
I own a tom cat who goes out by night
And brings his girl-friends back to share a bite.
They use the chairs (they're mostly full of moth),
Or leave black hairs and whiskers on the cloth.
A mass of Cupids hang around the hall;
The floor is freezing marble, wall-to-wall.

PASCOE POLGLAZE

Pascoe Polglaze, who tries so hard,
And rarely picks up an award,
Started the word game late in life,
Causing dismay to mates – and wife!
Oblivious of busts and beer,
Entirely lost in Comps; a seer
Perched upon a cromlech granite,
Old Pascoe's dreams are infinite:
Like using startling words – one week
'Gongoozle' might just do the trick!
Lacking Wordsworth's lyric urge,
And spouting metronomic dirge,
Zealously rhyming 'Mum' with 'Bum',
Each week he hopes his day will come!!!

ALISON PRINCE

Al,
Born in bloody Bromley.
Convention made Mother shudder. One should live for Art, she said,
    and Socialism.
(Dad played the piano with gloves on when it was cold.)
Ex-Slade,
Found living for Art tricky.
Got jobs sculpting blotting paper, feeding
Humans at Zoo,
Inventing telegrams as Cable and Wireless trainee,
Jokes get you the sack.
Kids more fun than grownups, so tried teaching.
Loved it, but
Married Welsh P.E. master.

No money, no job, three babies,
Oh, hell.
Perchance writing? T.V. lady said thirteen kiddiprogs,
Quick. Seven years of weekly comic strips and the Beeb
Resulted in latchkey teenagers, so fled to
Suffolk. Broke again. Reared pigs, calves,
Turkeys, milked cows, taught, wrote
Until escape fund and teenagers matured.
Vastly cheered, trotted off to Russia, China and such,
Wrote on and on, and moved to this island –
    and I'm not at the end, quite yet.

BASIL RANSOME-DAVIES

(SOUTHFORK. INT. NIGHT.)

J.R.:   Darling, I hear you're seeing this English fella, this Basil Ransome-
Davies. Now do you think that's wise?

SUE-ELLEN: It's nothing to do with you, J.R.

J.R.:   Well, that's just not so. After all, you are my wife. You know what
he is? He works in some college over in England, teaching literature
and all that stuff. Why, I hear he even scribbles poetry himself. It's
just downright humiliating to me to have you associate with someone
like that.

SUE-ELLEN: Of course you'd hate him, J.R. He's so – so sensitive.

J.R.:   Oh, I hear he gets real sensitive after a few drinks. I hear he's one
of these middle-aged hippy types with a big thirst and a small bank
balance.

SUE-ELLEN: Money isn't everything, J.R.

J.R.:   Well, I know one thing. The kind of money he makes from itty-
bitty magazines and suchlike isn't going to buy just one of those pretty
dresses of yours.

MARGARET MAYDAY ROGERS (b. 1921)

You may wonder why, September-born, her middle name's Mayday –
   Was her birth such a disaster for her folk?
Or somewhere was a revolution going on, full sway?
    Or was it just the Vicar's little joke?
    Her Ma was May Day born and so named, oke?

Margaret was born and bred and schooled in Sheffield, read
   English at the University;
Got a B.A. and a Dip.Ed. and an M.A. and got wed,
    Got a baby and began a Ph.D.:
    Then got polio, as tiresome as can be.

210

So instead of reading on, she taught foreigners galore
 And learned about their countries on the way.
Now she's doing her own thing and enjoys it more and more;
 And wins some in the *Statesman* as May Day:
 Perhaps that's really all there is to say.

RON RUBIN

§ And it came to pass in the days of Queen Victoria, that a man came
forth out of the land of Russia unto the city of the Scousemen, yea, even
unto Liverpool, and dwelt there. And he changed his name from Rubin
Sheroshevski to Sheroshevski Rubin, because some comedian told him
it sounded more English. And he begat sons and grandsons, one of
whom was called Ron, which is the whole point of this exercise.

§ And Ron waxed older and went to Liverpool College and to Law School
where he was exceedingly slothful, and far too interested in playing jazz
musick and generally larking about. And his teachers were wroth with
him, and there was a fair amount of gnashing of teeth. Wherefore Ron
arose and shook the dust of that city from off his feet, and became a
soldier in the army of the King. And when the prodigal returned, he
ministered unto his father as Chief Scribe for six summers. Then, one
day, behold, a Voice called unto him, saying: Hearken! get thine finger
out, Ron, and henceforth follow the True Path of jazz musick.

§ Now in those days the Scousites walked after strange gods that their
fathers knew not, and there was great tumult and twanging of guitars,
so that all those with healthy earholes were sore astonished.

§ Wherefore Ron girded up his loins and departed once more from the
city of his fathers. And he dwelt in the South with his wife who was of
the tribes of Ham and Japheth, yea, an Afro-Saxon woman. And they
were fruitful and multiplied and begat four children. And to this day
Ron playeth jazz musick upon the bass viol and the pianoforte. And thus
saith he: Verily, this is a damn sight more fun than working.

STANLEY J. SHARPLESS

I am an ex-executive, no jokes than mine are cleaner,
A former copywriter of unflappable demeanour,
Now happily retired from all those unforgiving deadlines,
The daily round of fabricating would-be-clever headlines.

For longer than I care to say, I've done the weekly comps,
Rejoicing in the challenge of those literary romps,
The prizes in my salad days – just like the skirts – were mini,
But fame and fortune beckoned every time I won a guinea.

Put out to grass in Dorset now, I scribble verse and prose,
For everybody from The Beeb to drill-hall village shows,
And in the intervals between, urged on by stick and carrot,
Contribute to anthologies compiled by Eric Parrott.

JOHN STANLEY SWEETMAN (b. 1922)

My name is Sweetman; by the silver Thames
I saw the light, then came to Basingstoke,
Whose Grammar School taught me the love of words;
A love not lost in five years soldiering,
Nor yet in forty more 'in paper'. Now
Retired from toil I tend my garden plot,
Do Literary Competitions and campaign
For Christian Unity in God's good time,
A Catholic ecumaniac. From
A happy marriage over forty years
Came half-a-dozen children and, from these,
Fifteen, to date, of grandchildren, some of whom,
Though young, put pen to paper with some skill.

PETER VEALE

Mr Veale, the only thing people know about you is that Edward Heath, your head boy at school in Ramsgate, told you off for being improperly dressed. Did the future Prime Minister say anything else to you?
He told me to pull myself together. For a half-century or so since then I've been proving that I can't. Another of his failures, I suppose.
Anything else of interest ever happened to you?
Well, when I was in the Army I had my wallet stolen by a policeman – in a Middle Eastern country which I won't name for fear of repercussions.
Anything more remarkable than that?
Yes, I got the wallet back with the money still in it.
I suppose you have earned a living in some way?
Yes, as a reporter and sub-editor on newspapers, including The Sun. *To do that sort of thing you have to be a parodist.*

N. J. WARBURTON

. . . The chums waited while Dick downed as much pop as he could and tucked into a plate of buns.

'I've found out about that mysterious stranger,' he informed them at last.

'Do tell!' they all yelled.

'Well,' responded Dick, lowering his voice, 'he comes from Cambridge but he's jolly well nothing to do with the University. Far from it. He was born in Woodford, in 1947.'

'I knew there was something shifty about him,' Jane interjected.

'That's not all, though,' continued Dick. 'He went to school there and then he went off to become a teacher!'

'The blighter!' chorused the twins. 'We ought to get him back for that.'

'After that,' persisted Dick, 'he packed it in to try writing for the wireless.'

There was a pause while the pals looked at each other.

'Is that it?' demanded Jane.

'Yes,' intoned Dick with a sidelong glance at the remaining bun.

'A bit boring for an adventure, isn't it?' queried Jane.

LT.-COL. W. F. N. WATSON (alias Adam Khan,
Tom Brewer, William Hodson, Richard Probyn, James Skinner,
F. Galway, et al.)

When you consider how his life was spent,
A soldier of three Kings and Our Dear Queen,
In Europe, Near East and the Raj he's been,
In barrack, camp, cantonment, quarters, tent,
You'd really wonder, after thirty years
'Mid brutal and licentious soldiery,
Mere hunting, shooting, cricket devotee,
What *were* the Muses thinking of, poor dears,
Recruiting *him* to illustrate a mix
Of diverse books, and ruling next that he
Should Questions write for University
Challenge – 10,000 odd by '86,
And draw cartoons, win competitions, viz.
Spectator, Statesman, Punch, and also write
For Krypton Factor and such Quiz Shows bright
As Cabbages and Kings and Ultra Quiz.
Now 1986, the apogee;
His Golden Wedding Anniversary.

DILYS WAVISH

I was a convent pupil taught
By nuns, I quite enjoyed it,
Except when we had algebra
When I tried to avoid it.

At sweet sixteen I left and trained
To be a secretary,
A civil servant I became,
To work was necessary.

In my spare time I scribbled hard
And wrote a thrilling story
In which a madman stalked his prey;
It was distinctly gory!

From that day on I've not looked back.
Now I'm a published writer,
But sad to say it doesn't pay
My purse is now much lighter!

BRENDA WHINCUP

WANTED – DEAD OR ALIVE

Brenda Whincup, rumoured to be still lurking in London although she is known to be seeking an escape to Shropshire, is A.W.O.L. – absent without literature. The most recent sighting of her can be found in the pages of an American quarterly, and a stake-out should be maintained on a forthcoming Aberdeen University Press anthology. Her *modus operandi* can be studied in back issues of *The Master Craftsman* and sundry other magazines. Out on parole she received a gold medal, for good behaviour, at last year's Cambridge Festival.

However, her recent low level of productivity has induced her fear that not only is she an ex-nurse and ex-actress but, possibly, an ex-human being too. Anyone who can help her to locate her once creative *alter ego* could be considered for a £5 million reward.

WHAT THEY WROTE

ACKNOWLEDGEMENTS

The following items, either in whole or in part, first appeared in the Weekend Competition pages of the *New Statesman*:

    'Dylan Thomas' by Alison Prince

    'Anne Hathaway', 'Sir John Betjeman', and 'Philip Larkin' all by Stanley J. Sharpless.

I would like to express my thanks to all contributors for their co-operation and patience, and especially to those who failed to gain any acceptances. There was so much competition that rejection was inevitable for a large number of entries.

I would also like to thank Mike Rees, the librarian of Havering Technical College, for checking dates and other material when I was temporarily out of range of a reference library; Jonathan Barker and other helpful staff at the Arts Council Poetry Library; Derek Jenkinson of the R.N.I.B. for assistance with technical aid to enable me to read the contributions; Mark Le Fanu of the Society of Authors for some very timely assistance; Tricia Parrott, my wife, without whose constant assistance my books would never see the light of day.

ALPHABETICAL INDEX
OF BIOGRAPHIES